Julie Smith
1981

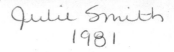

RESEARCH TECHNIQUES FOR CLINICAL SOCIAL WORKERS

RESEARCH TECHNIQUES FOR CLINICAL SOCIAL WORKERS

Tony Tripodi and Irwin Epstein

1980
COLUMBIA UNIVERSITY PRESS
NEW YORK

Library of Congress Cataloging in Publication Data

Tripodi, Tony.
Research techniques for clinical social workers.

Includes bibliographies and index.
1. Social service—Research. I. Epstein, Irwin,
joint author. II. Title.
HV11.T747   361'.0072   80-15516
ISBN 0-231-04652-9

Columbia University Press
New York   Guildford, Surrey

To
Philomena Torchia Halstead
and
Kayla Conrad

CONTENTS

ACKNOWLEDGMENTS

We wish to thank our many colleagues and research students, too numerous to mention, who have stimulated us to write this book. Moreover, we are thankful to Cheryl Dunny and Debbie Moorehead for their typing and clerical assistance on the original manuscript; and to John Moore, our editor, and Phillip Fellin, dean of the University of Michigan, School of Social Work, for their encouragement.

Tony Tripodi
Irwin Epstein

RESEARCH TECHNIQUES FOR CLINICAL SOCIAL WORKERS

1

PURPOSE OF THE BOOK

The purpose of this book is to provide an introduction to the use of research concepts and techniques for collecting, analyzing, and interpreting information relevant to clinical social work practice. By the latter, we refer to the efforts of social caseworkers and groupworkers to help individuals, families and groups of clients to resolve their psycho/social problems. These efforts may involve changing the clients, changing others in the client's environment, or both. They take place in a range of organizational settings and are rooted in a variety of theoretical perspectives.

The book is written for social work students and practitioners who are not research trained. It presents selected social research concepts and techniques that can be applied by clinical social workers irrespective of their theoretical orientations or practice settings. Accordingly, examples will be provided throughout the book which incorporate different practice theories and different programmatic locations. Neither the research concepts and techniques, nor the practice theories and settings are exhaustive. They simply represent a beginning attempt to incorporate research into clinical social work practice.

Our basic assumption in writing this book is that the use of social research concepts and techniques can facilitate the rational use of information by social workers engaged in direct practice with individuals, families, and groups. Our emphasis, however, is on the collection and use of information concerning individual clients and "significant others" in their lives. Consequently, we employ primarily concepts which treat the individual as the basic unit of analysis. And while we do not utilize concepts which focus on the family or group, *per se*, such as family power structure or group cohesiveness, we do indicate how clients involved in family therapy or group treatment can be clinically assessed as individuals. Moreover, we suggest ways in which individual data can be aggregated or combined to make inferences about families and groups.

NEED FOR THE BOOK

Although research courses are required in any social work curriculum, clinically oriented social work students tend to view these courses as irrelevant to practice. Often they are. As a result, many practicing social workers, who have merely "done their time" in required research courses fail to see how research can aid them in their work. When they do recognize its potential utility, often they do not know how to put research into their practice.

Despite their lack of applied research training and competence, practicing social workers are under increasing pressure from funding sources, client groups, and agency administrators for more objective information describing their efforts and their effectiveness. In addition, the more professionally oriented practitioners undoubtedly are aware of the increasing interest in "research-based-practice" within the social work profession itself.* This interest is reflective of a desire on the part of some social work researchers to

---

* See, for example, S. Jarayatne and R. Levy, *Empirical Clinical Practice* (New York: Columbia University Press, 1979); S. Briar, "Incorporating Research into Education for Clinical Practice in Social Work: Toward a Clinical Science in Social Work," in *Proceeding of the Conference on Research Utilization in Social Work Education* (New York: Council on Social Work Education, 1977).

develop a systematic, research validated, knowledge base for practice.

Our effort is intended to make research more applicable to practice. Without assuming a high level of research sophistication on the part of the reader, the book will describe ways in which "line" social workers and their supervisors can use research to improve the quality of information they collect and thereby improve the quality of practice decisions they make.

To achieve this end, we make use of a strategy similar to one we employed in our previous book, *Research Techniques for Program Planning, Monitoring, and Evaluation.* That book was written for program planners and administrators and attempted to apply research concepts and techniques to administrative practice. Many of our colleagues have encouraged us to direct the same strategy towards clinical social work practice. More specifically, our approach involves: conceptualizing and dividing practice into parts in which major tasks are performed; delineating practice objectives within each practice division; identifying research concepts and techniques that can be employed to achieve these objectives; describing the principles and procedures involved in using these concepts and techniques; providing illustrations of their use in practice situations; and, finally, demonstrating how the information they generate can inform practice decisions.

FORMAT

Our conception of clinical social work practice and the book itself are divided into three sections: diagnostic assessment and treatment formulation; treatment implementation and monitoring; and evaluation. These divisions reflect critical areas of decision making in clinical practice and are consistent with many existing models of casework and groupwork practice. Thus, they closely parallel the "problem solving model" articulated in Compton and Galloway's book, *Social Work Processes.* Our conceptualization is also consistent with the practice skill areas identified in *Social Work Practice* by

Pincus and Minahan. Both texts are widely used introductions to social work practice.

More broadly, a review of current social work theories concerning individuals, families and groups suggests that these conceptual divisions describe major components in a wide variety of theoretical approaches such as ego psychology, behavior modification, case advocacy, task-centered casework, psychosocial practice in small groups, and group problem-solving approaches. It should be emphasized, however, that we are not arguing that all aspects of clinical social work can be reduced to this three part conceptualization. Nor are we saying that all clinical practice is reduceable to research techniques. Nonetheless, our three part division makes useful distinctions between different aspects of practice in each of the foregoing practice theories. It is also "heuristic" in that it makes it easier to envision possible applications of research concepts and techniques to direct practice.

Diagnostic assessment and treatment formulation involves decisions about the nature and extent of a client's problem; whether the client is adequately motivated for involvement in a social work process, etc. Treatment implementation and monitoring refers to that phase of practice in which judgements are made about the extent to which the client is actually receiving the prescribed intervention in a manner which is consistent with professional standards, the practicing social worker's initial planning and the contractual understanding between client and social worker. Evaluation refers to decisions about the effectiveness and efficiency with which the clinical objectives are attained and whether treatment should be intensified, reduced, or terminated.

Within the three major sections of the book, chapters will present suggested uses of selected research concepts and techniques for assessment, implementation and evaluation. Although a technique may be introduced in the context of one of these functions, its use may not be confined to that function. Thus, for example, standardized interviewing techniques are introduced in the section devoted to client assessment. Clearly, however, these techniques can be applied to monitoring and evaluation as well. Each chapter provides principles for implementing a given technique and hypothetical examples of how the technique can be applied to actual practice situations. This is followed by an applied research exercise for the reader. A selected bibliography ends each chapter.

Rather than being exhaustive in our survey of research methods, we have selected those which we believe can be learned easily and readily applied by social work students and practitioners. By our applying these methods to a broad range of practice examples, our intent is to show that the incorporation of research into casework and groupwork practice need not be bound to any particular theoretical approach or agency setting.

INTENDED USE

This book is intended for use as an introductory research text for graduate casework, groupwork and generic social work students. It also can be used as a supplementary text for direct practice courses along with basic practice texts such as the aforementioned books by Compton and Galloway and by Pincus and Minahan. Finally, the book is intended for practicing social workers who value the increased integration of social research into their social work practice.

SELECTED BIBLIOGRAPHY

Compton, Beulah Roberts and Burt Galloway, eds., *Social Work Processes* (Homewood, Ill.: Dorsey Press, 1975), chs. 6–11.

Epstein, Irwin and Tony Tripodi, *Research Techniques for Program Planning, Monitoring, and Evaluation* (New York: Columbia University Press, 1977), pp. 1–3, 5–8, 55–58, and 111–16.

Pincus, Allen and Anne Minahan, *Social Work Practice: Model and Method* (Itasca, Ill.; F. E. Peacock, 1973), chs. 6–13.

Roberts, Robert W. and Helen Northen, eds., *Theories of Social Work with Groups* (New York: Columbia University Press, 1976), chs. 3, 4, 8, and 11.

Tripodi, Tony, *Uses and Abuses of Social Research in Social Work* (New York: Columbia University Press, 1974), pp. 122–31.

Tripodi, Tony, Phillip Fellin, Irwin Epstein, and Roger Lind, eds., *Social Workers at Work: An Introduction to Social Work Practice* (2d Edition; Itasca, Ill.: F. E. Peacock, 1977), pp. 63–160.

Turner, Francis J., ed., *Social Work Treatment: Interlocking Theoretical Approaches* (New York: Free Press, 1974), chs. 3, 5, 8, 13, and 15.

Part One

ASSESSING THE PROBLEM AND FORMULATING THE TREATMENT

Diagnostic assessment and treatment formulation is the first phase of clinical social work practice. It involves a number of interrelated tasks and decisions for the social worker. In this section, we describe these tasks and decisions and discuss, rather generally, the ways in which research can inform them. The following four chapters describe in greater detail the use of specific research concepts and techniques in client assessment and in the formulation of treatment plans and objectives.

TASKS

As we indicated above, diagnostic assessment and treatment formulation require that the clinical social worker accomplish a number of tasks and make a number of decisions. These tasks are as follows:

1. First, the social worker must obtain information from the potential client, the referral source if there is one, and significant others in the potential client's life to determine the nature and extent of his/her problem. Sometimes the potential client is quite capable of precisely defining the problem and its source. S/he may require help in finding employment, child management, and so on. At other times, the potential client may offer a more ambiguous and diffuse statement of his/her problem. S/he may experience feel-

ings of meaninglessness or anxiety which s/he cannot explain or control. The latter form of "presenting problem" requires more active involvement on the part of the social worker in specifying those problems which require or allow social work intervention.

Whatever form the presenting problem takes, the task is to make an appropriate initial assessment of the potential client's social, psychological, economic and health needs as well as of his/her requests or demands for service. In cases in which the potential client does not present him/herself voluntarily for treatment, such as those encountered in prisons, nonvoluntary mental hospital admissions and the like, the social worker must still secure enough information from the potential client to make a reasonable and humane assessment of his/her needs.

2. The second major task for the clinical social worker is to determine whether the potential client meets the eligibility requirements imposed on clients by the social agency and its funding sources. Equally important, is to determine whether the services provided by the agency are appropriate to the client's problem. The former, determining eligibility, may require information about income, place of residence, age, marital status, and other demographics. The latter, determining whether the services offered are most appropriate, requires not only a knowledge of the potential client's need, but information as well about the full range of services offered by the agency, those services available from other agencies in the potential client's environment, and information about those values, beliefs, attitudes, abilities and deficiencies which might affect the potential client's utilization of the available services. Fulfilling these information requirements may involve contact with a variety of sources in the potential client's environment such as other social agencies, schools, places of employment, and so on. Whatever the source, the information gathered must be reliable enough to serve as a basis for decision-making.

3. Once it has been determined that the potential client can benefit from what the social worker and the agency have to offer,

some further specification must take place. This specification involves refining information about the causes or etiology of the potential client's problem. Explanations may come from clinical research and/or from the potential client him/herself. They may come from individuals in the potential client's environment such as relatives, physicians, teachers, and the like. Whatever the source, the available information must be sifted and sorted in order to determine an appropriate target or targets of social work intervention.

4. Very likely, there will be more than one "cause" and more than one problem. A physically abused child, for example, may be having trouble in school, living in inadequate housing, in need of medical or psychiatric attention, and so on. His/her parents may be unemployed, without funds, alcoholic and lacking adequate child management skills. In such cases, priorities must be set. Even the most skillful and dedicated social worker cannot intervene on all fronts at the same time. Moreover, clients cannot productively engage in a social work process if they are trying to solve all their problems at once. Consequently, information must be gathered concerning the most "proximate" or direct causes of the potential client's problems and his/her own priorities concerning which of these is most pressing and requires most immediate attention. In the case of physical abuse one must first attend to medical needs and the need for protection from future abuse before confronting some of the possible causes.

5. Once priorities have been set, the social worker must determine the kind and extent of social work intervention or treatment that is called for. We use the term "treatment" here in its broadest sense to include any of a number of possible helping strategies. These strategies are aptly summarized by Pincus and Minahan (see bibliography) as: *therapy*, helping the client to achieve desired psychosocial changes in terms of attitudes, behaviors, and moods; *education*, increasing the client's knowledge and skills; *advocacy*, locating and securing resources for the client and/or representing the client in attempts to change his/her environment; *care*, helping

clients to seek and secure basic human needs such as housing, food, employment, and the like; and, *referral*, helping clients to seek appropriate services from other health and social agencies.

In the child-abuse case mentioned earlier, the social worker may, in the course of treatment, employ each of these strategies. The child may receive therapy. The parent may receive education concerning less destructive techniques of child management. The social worker may advocate for the family for emergency public welfare benefits and help the family find adequate housing. In addition, the social worker might refer the alcoholic parent to a treatment facility or a self-help organization.

6. With treatment objectives specified and prioritized and with the intervention strategies tentatively chosen, the social worker can establish a "contract" or working agreement with the potential client concerning treatment goals and mutual obligations in seeking these goals or objectives. In some social agencies, this contract is a formal written statement of treatment goals and mutual obligations. In others, the contract is oral and informal. Nevertheless, if treatment is to be successful, a mutual understanding of goals, rights and obligations must be arrived at. This consensus between worker and potential client may require negotiation about goal priorities and means for achieving them. Thus, for example, a newly divorced woman may want help finding a job before she is willing to confront her feelings of depression. The social worker may prefer it the other way around. Once these differences are resolved, the "potential" client has become a client and the social worker and/or social agency has accepted a commitment to provide service.

7. After the contract has been agreed to, a final task remains. This involves "operationalization" of treatment objectives and the means for achieving them. In other words, the social worker must clearly articulate what s/he is trying to achieve and how s/he will try to achieve it. This should be done in precise enough language so that it would be possible to determine whether the client is actually receiving the kind and amount of treatment contracted for and whether the intended outcomes have been achieved by the time

treatment terminates. The specification of the amount and kind of treatment required makes treatment monitoring possible. The specification of treatment objectives is required for evaluation. Both, however, are necessary "planning" aspects of the diagnostic assessment and treatment formulation phase of clinical practice.

So, for example, a school social worker may constitute a group of children whose disruptive behaviors are keeping them in trouble in school and interfering with their learning. S/he will specify the number and characteristics of the youngsters in the group, how often they will meet and for how long, the treatment or groupwork techniques to be used and the intended goals for each child in terms of reduction of disruptive behavior and increase in educational achievement. By carefully specifying means and ends, it is now possible to monitor and evaluate group treatment.

ASSESSMENT AND TREATMENT DECISIONS

Clinical social workers make many crucial decisions during the process of diagnostic assessment and treatment formulation. As much as possible, these decisions should be guided by complete and factual information. Often, however, crisis situations and agency pressures deny the social worker the luxury of enough time to do a full psychosocial study. Here, previous experience with similar cases, intuition, knowledge of relevant research studies and consultation with colleagues or supervisors can supplement the social worker's ability to correctly diagnose and effectively intervene.

In situations in which the social worker cannot gather full and complete information before intervening, the skilled clinician recognizes that s/he is basing his/her treatment decisions on a "working hypothesis" about the client's problem, its causes and its solution. This tentative hypothesis is validated, refined or totally rejected in the course of treatment as new information about the client's situation emerges. For this reason, the process of diagnostic assessment and treatment formulation can continue throughout the actual implementation of treatment.

Whether diagnostic and treatment decisions are made prior to or during the treatment process, certain questions must be answered about the client and his/her problems if effective intervention is to take place. Some of these questions are as follows:

1. Who is the client? What are his/her social and psychological attributes?
2. How and why did the client come into contact with the agency?
3. What are the client's problems and can they be ameliorated through social work intervention?
4. Is the client motivated to participate in a social work process?
5. What are the treatment objectives?
6. What intervention strategies and techniques should be employed?
7. Are the social worker and client in agreement about treatment objectives and the means to achieve these?

SOME QUALIFIERS AND ASSUMPTIONS

Although seven steps have been presented in describing the tasks involved in diagnostic assessment and treatment formulation and seven decisions have been listed above, it should be clear that seven is not presented as a magic number and ours is not a magic formulation. Thus, many different models exist which describe the first phase of treatment. We have simply tried to reduce these models to a set of abstractions which hopefully captures their essentials.

Moreover, while we have described these tasks in a neat, logical order, practice may not conform to our rational model. Thus, for example, information necessary for more than one task may be gathered during one interview. Contracting may require going back and securing more basic information. And, as we indicated earlier, additional diagnostic information may be gathered after treatment begins. The process that actually takes place may be more like a circle or a spiral than the straight line which our model implies. The most important issue here, however, is arriving at an appropriate set of intervention objectives and strategies which are agreeable to the client and which are likely to be effective. The route the social worker takes in getting there is much less important.

Finally, our model assumes that clinical social workers will be knowledgeable enough and sufficiently "eclectic" to choose from the most effective and efficient intervention strategies to achieve treatment objectives. This assumption may be unrealistic. Some social workers, for example, are bound by real limits in competence, by their own treatment preferences, and by therapeutic or ideological dogmatism. Social agencies may offer some kinds of treatment and proscribe others. Therefore, rather than a description of what is, our model represents a rational ideal which may be approximated in the course of social work history, but never really reached. Nonetheless, it is based on a value of rationality and effectiveness which the authors unashamedly endorse.

RESEARCH CONCEPTS AND TECHNIQUES

Sound diagnostic assessment and treatment formulation are dependent upon information that accurately portrays the client's situation. Research concepts and techniques can increase the quality and quantity of information gathered as well as improve the interpretation of this information. Three key research concepts that directly relate to the adequacy and accuracy of information are *reliability*, *validity*, and *representativeness*. Reliability refers to the extent to which the information gathered is internally consistent. (Does the client say contradictory things about him/herself?) Validity concerns the accuracy of the information. (Is there objective evidence to support the client's assertions?) Representativeness, involves the extent to which the information gathered is idiosyncratic and biased. (Are the client's assertions about his/her situation based on typical or unique events?).

These concepts will be discussed in greater detail as they relate to specific research techniques for gathering information necessary for diagnostic assessment and treatment formulation. In chapter 2, for example, we demonstrate the use of standardized research interviewing for gathering reliable, valid, and representative information from potential clients about their needs and problems. This technique is particularly useful in securing a potential client's self-assessment.

In addition to a self-assessment from the potential client, the social worker may desire an independent diagnostic assessment utilizing one or more of the many diagnostic instruments already available. In chapter 3, we discuss how social workers can locate these clinical assessment instruments and make judgements about the reliability, validity, representativeness, and usefulness of the information they generate.

Chapter 4 introduces another information gathering research technique, systematic observation. This technique is particularly useful in making diagnostic assessment based on the potential client's social interactions in "natural" settings such as at home, in school, and so on. Here again, the key concepts of reliability, validity, and representativeness are employed.

Chapter 5 identifies principles for choosing from among available intervention strategies. We discuss the research concepts of efficiency and effectiveness. In this context, reliability, validity and representativeness also play a role in making judgements about which intervention strategies to employ.

SELECTED BIBLIOGRAPHY

Epstein, Irwin and Tony Tripodi, *Research Techniques for Program Planning, Monitoring, and Evaluation* (New York: Columbia University Press, New York, 1977), chs. 3, 4, and 5.

Ciminero, Anthony R., Karen S. Calhoun, and Henry E. Adams, eds., *Handbook of Behavioral Assessment* (New York: Wiley, 1977), pp. 3–15.

Compton, Beulah R., and Burt Galloway, eds., *Social Work Processes* (Homewood, Ill.: Dorsey Press, 1975), chs. 7 and 8.

Gottman, John M., and Sandra R. Leiblum, *How To Do Psychotherapy and How to Evaluate It* (New York: Holt, Rinehart, and Winston, 1974), ch. 3.

Pincus, Allen and Anne Minahan, *Social Work Practice: Model and Method* (Itasca, Ill.: F. E. Peacock, 1973), chs. 6–9.

Tripodi, Tony, *Uses and Abuses of Social Research in Social Work* (New York: Columbia University Press, 1974), pp. 124–27.

Tripodi, Tony, Phillip Fellin, Irwin Epstein, and Roger Lind, *Social Workers at Work: An Introduction to Social Work Practice* (2d ed.; Itasca, Ill.: F. E. Peacock, 1977), pp. 64–71.

2

RESEARCH INTERVIEWING AND QUESTIONNAIRES

The research interview is perhaps the most powerful and versatile of techniques for gathering information directly from another person. Routinely, it involves a face-to-face exchange between the person seeking information and the person giving it. It may also take place over the telephone. Whether in person or over the phone, successful interviewing requires that the interviewer give a good deal of attention to the research instrument as well as to his/her role in the interview situation. The interviewer's primary goal is to gather relevant data by encouraging, facilitating and guiding the respondent to provide unbiased and unambiguous answers to necessary questions.

Interviews may vary from relatively *unstructured* formats to *semi-structured* to *highly structured* ones. A highly structured interview is organized according to themes or topics and presents the respondent with a set of specific questions which the interviewer reads aloud. The answer categories are also structured, so that the respondent must choose from a set of predesignated or *forced-choice* response categories. In this type of interview, the interview situation is *standardized* as well. Hence, there are explicit instructions for the interviewer to follow regarding the location of the interview, its duration, and even things to say when the respondent is having difficulty answering. Consequently, the structured interview is characterized by a high degree of control over both the interviewer and the respondent. In addition, it offers a high degree of consistency from one interview to another. Some interview schedules are so highly structured that they permit the respondent to interview him/herself. These are called *self-administered questionnaires*.

At the other end of the continuum is the unstructured interview. This approach is best suited for studying highly sensitive or unexplored subjects in depth. Rather than offering the respondent forced-choice response categories, the unstructured interview presents open-ended questions to respondents which they may answer as they please. The interviewer is also free to rephrase questions and to use whatever supportive or probing comments are necessary to elicit desired information. This technique demands great sensitivity to the respondent's feelings, attitudes and opinions as well as to his/her nonverbal behavior. Although the unstructured interview involves little control over the interviewer and respondent, the interview situation cannot go unattended. To be successful, an unstructured interview must take place in surroundings that are physically comfortable and free from distraction or stress.

Somewhere between these extremes is the semi-structured interview. It usually involves some combination of open-ended and forced-choice questions. Within specified limits, the interviewer may rephrase questions or probe responses. The interviewer's task, however, is to keep the respondent focused on particular issues and questions. As a result, s/he exercises more control over the direction of the interview than in an unstructured interview.

Whatever the type of interview, successful information retrieval requires that respondents understand the questions, be motivated to answer them honestly, and be knowledgeable about the matters covered in the interview. Moreover, the interviewer should conduct him/herself in a friendly but professional manner and show interest in and knowledge about the topics discussed. Most important, s/he should be nonjudgmental and accepting of the opinions and information offered by the respondent.

INTERVIEWING AND DIAGNOSTIC ASSESSMENT

Diagnostic assessment requires reliable and valid information about the type and severity of the client's problem, the need for treatment or for some other form of intervention, the level of client motivation, and so on. Social workers have traditionally employed "clinical interviewing" to secure this information. This form of interviewing is most akin to what researchers refer to as unstructured interviewing. It is flexible, sensitive and attuned to verbal as well as nonverbal client behavior.

Although clinical interviewing has been used historically by social workers and is well formulated within particular modes of social work practice, it has its limitations as well. Thus, by tending to focus on unique aspects of the client's situation, the clinical interview may ignore elements which are common to many clients. This "blind spot" may prevent the evaluation of the progress of whole classes of clients through the accumulation of information about them. Moreover, it may obscure intervention possibilities aimed at more than the individual client. Finally, clinical interviewing takes a lot of time, motivation and emotional investment on the part of the interviewer and respondent alike. Often, agency conditions and client crisis situations make in-depth clinical interviewing an unrealistic and inefficient mode of information gathering.

More structured and standardized research interviewing procedures are well codified and documented in the social research literature. While these procedures do not generate information with the richness and depth of clinical interview protocols, research interviews are more efficient and consistent in the information they produce. They can be employed at intake for diagnostic assessment, during treatment for monitoring purposes, and after treatment has terminated for evaluation. These standardized techniques also may be introduced into clinical interviews as a supplement for gathering less sensitive factual information. However there are times when the information-gathering purposes of a standardized interview may have to be compromised for the sake of clinical demands.

PRINCIPLES OF RESEARCH AND DIAGNOSTIC INTERVIEWING

1. The Purpose of the Interview

In conducting a research interview or an intake interview, one should be clear about the reasons for wanting to conduct it, the kind of information to be gathered, the characteristics of the respondents, the role of the interviewer, and the character of the interview setting. For the clinical social worker, this means fitting the interview to the context of the social agency in which s/he is employed. More specifically, the social worker will want to know how and why the applicant came to the agency for help, how s/he defines the problem or need, whether the potential client's problems will be ameliorated by the services that the agency offers, whether the applicant is eligible for those services, and so on.

To facilitate trust and openness, the respondent should be told in a few brief introductory comments, the purpose of the interview, why the information is desired, and how it will be used. Respondents are most cooperative when they can be assured of confidentiality. In addition, questions should be limited to areas which are relevant for diagnostic and/or intervention decisions.

2. The Content of the Interview Schedule

The interview schedule or questionnaire has two basic functions: it serves as a guide to the interviewer and poses the questions to respondents. In diagnostic interviewing, the content of the interview schedule should be consistent with the theoretical point of view of the social worker and the agency s/he represents. Questions posed should provide the social worker with the information that is required to make sound diagnostic and interventive decisions *within* his/her theoretical framework. Thus, for example, a clinical social worker operating within a "systems" framework will require information about a number of different systems in which the potential client is implicated such as work, family, school, and peers. A social worker in an advocacy agency may be concerned primarily with questions about a potential client's relationship to a particular agency which has failed to provide legal entitlements. In psychiatric settings using psychodynamic treatment models, diagnostic interviews are more likely to focus on developmental histories of patients. Irrespective of which theoretical framework is employed, however, it is essential that questions asked are consistent with it.

Having considered the interviewer's need for information, we now turn our attention to the respondent. First, since a primary function of diagnostic interviewing is to elicit the potential client's perception of his/her needs, problems and his/her perceptions of their causes and solutions, the language and syntax of the questions should correspond to that of the respondent. More generally, the questions should be clear, unbiased and each focused on a single thought or issue.

3. The Structure of the Interview

Most research interviews move from the general to the specific. This is called a *funnel approach*. It begins with general, nonthreatening, orienting questions and gradually leads to more specific, detailed ones. As we indicated earlier, highly structured interviews may contain instructions to the interviewer for rephrasing questions that are not receiving clear, complete or relevant responses. This attempt to standardize the interviewer's language increases the chances that information gathered from different respondents will be comparable. A marital therapist, for example, will want to ask husband and wife exactly the same questions about their marital problems in separate interviews. If questions were posed differently to the two respondents, differences in response might be more a consequence of the ways in which the questions were asked than a reflection of conflicting perceptions of the marital partners.

Moreover, if husband and wife are interviewed by different social workers, the workers should be trained through direct instruction and role-playing techniques so that their interviewing behavior is similar. Finally, if any useful generalizations are to be made about the kinds of problems people are bringing to the agency, the questions asked at intake must be standardized from worker to worker and from case to case. This standardization is equally important in monitoring and evaluating client progress.

Sometimes, during the course of an interview, respondents may give vague, partially circular, or irrelevant responses. A technique for encouraging respondents to clarify their responses is *probing*. Probing is "continued neutral questioning" that has the purpose of either clarifying responses or redirecting the respondent to answer a question more precisely. Some examples of common interviewer's probes are: "In what way?" "Could you explain that in more detail?" "What do you mean by that?" Or, a simple reflective probe might be used. Here the interviewer repeats the respondent's last few words or a key phrase from a preceding response in a questioning manner. The respondent is thereby encouraged to expand on his/her previous response.

Ideally, the interview should not exceed an hour. Interviews beyond an hour are exhausting for the interviewer and respondent alike. In certain agencies, e.g., in-patient mental hospitals, residential child-care institutions, and the like, multiple interviews are possible if the necessary information cannot be gathered in one sitting. In settings in which clients come and go voluntarily, more than one intake interview is likely to substantially reduce the chances that the applicant client will return. Whatever the setting, however, the interview should be as efficient as possible and confined to essential information gathering. Semistructured and structured interviews promote this kind of efficiency.

The interview should conclude with the interviewer briefly summarizing how s/he plans to use the information given and offering the respondent an opportunity to make any brief additional comments about issues covered or neglected in the interview. Since future contact with the respondent may occur, it is important that positive rapport be maintained throughout the interview and that the respondent feel that his/her self-revelation and openness has been appreciated. In addition, the concluding comments made by the respondent may serve as a useful bridge or connecting theme for the next interview.

4. *The Interview Schedule*

In constructing an interview schedule, the social worker should list the types of information necessary and pertinent to the purpose of the interview. After this list has been prepared, topics should be ranked in order of importance. Finally, the list should be pared down so that the interview itself would not be excessively long.

Having identified the areas to be covered, the social worker must then decide how structured the interview should be. The semistructured interview specifies the types of information sought and leaves the respondent free to answer in his/her own way. The structured interview, on the other hand, specifies the types of information sought, the specific questions to be asked, and even provides the choice of available responses to these questions. In general, more structured questions are best for gathering factual information which is not emotionally charged. When the range of responses to these questions is well known, closed-ended questions should be provided. Semistructured, open-ended questions are best for eliciting expressions of emotion, personal need, and answers to questions in areas in which the social worker and/or the agency have little previous knowledge of response possibilities.

Interviews need not be completely structured or completely lacking in structure. In fact, some combination of structure and flexibility is often preferable. Moreover, as knowledge and experience are accumulated, interview formats may be revised and become more structured over time.

If a semistructured format is employed, the basic dimensions to be covered in the interview are specified and examples of questions and probes which the interviewer may use are provided. For example, a dimension to be explored might be the potential client's "presenting problem." Questions might be formulated about what s/he sees as the reason s/he came to the agency, why s/he chose this agency, what services s/he hopes to receive, and so on.

Although the funnel approach, moving from the general to the specific is always used in structured interviews and frequently used in semistructured interviews, the latter may follow a format that is referred to as an *umbrella approach*. In this format, instead of moving from general to specific, the interviewer comprehensively covers all facets of a given dimension exhaustively. The respondent is given a chance to raise any additional thought s/he might have in relation to this dimension before moving to the next dimension. The umbrella approach helps to define the broad parameters of a problem, but can lead to the collection of information that is never utilized. Alternatively, the funnel approach is especially useful for approaching sensitive topics gradually yet ultimately retrieving detailed information.

In formulating questions for structured and semistructured interviews, four general principles should be followed: (1) questions should be clearly stated; (2) questions should not reflect biases of the interviewer; (3) each question should contain one thought only; and (4) questions should flow in a logical order. The art of asking questions is to ask them simply and concisely in understandable language and in a logical sequence.

Once questions have been written, a decision must be made about the degree to which responses will be structured. Should questions be open-ended or closed? As we indicated earlier, open-ended questions require less advance knowledge about the kinds of responses the questions are likely to elicit. However, responses to these questions can get out of hand sometimes and respondents can digress widely from the topics to be covered. Closed questions require advance knowledge about the range of responses likely and are preferable for collecting straightforward and behaviorally specific data.

The following list indicates some of the various response systems available for what is basically the same question about parent/child problems.

   a. The open-ended question:
      1. Can you tell me something about any problems you are having with your children? (Respondent answers in any way s/he chooses).
   b. Closed questions:
      1. Simple "yes" or "no."
         Do you have problems with your children? Yes ____ No ____
      2. Frequency of occurrence (adverb modifiers).
         How often do you have problems with your children? Always ____ Almost always ____ Occasionally ____ Rarely ____ Never ____
      3. Frequency of occurrence (numerical).
         How often do you have problems with your children? Daily ____ About every other day ____ Two to three times a week ____ About once a week ____
      4. Frequency of occurrence (percentage).
         How often do you have problems with your children? 0–10% of the time ____ 11–50% of the time ____ Over 50% of the time ____
      5. Agree/Disagree scales.
         Indicate how much you agree with the following statement: I often have problems with my children. Strongly agree ____ Agree ____ Disagree ____ Strongly disagree ____
      6. Comparative response scales.
         Compared to other problems you now have, how important are the problems with your children? Very important ____ Somewhat important ____ Unimportant ____

The foregoing are only a few of the response formats that one can use. Others include rank ordering problems the respondent has, asking the respondent to identify his/her problems from a list of problems, or asking the respondent to rate the intensity of a given problem on a numerical scale from 1 to 10, and so on.

In selecting response systems one should choose those that appear to be most appropriate to the interview and to typical respondents. Complicated systems should not be used when a simple "yes" or "no" would suffice. For closed-ended questions, a few additional rules apply to the construction of response alternatives. First, response categories should be *mutually exclusive*. This means that for any given question the answer given should fit in one and only one response category. In other words, the categories may not overlap. In addition response categories should *exhaust* the range of possible responses. Wherever possible, one should avoid the use of noncommittal response categories such as "Undecided," "Don't know," and the like. These options discourage thoughtful deliberation on the part of the respondent in answering difficult or sensitive questions. Finally, in constructing an interview schedule, it is preferable to choose one or two types of response systems that are readily understood by most respondents. Excessive variation of the response system leads to confusion, fatigue, and unreliable information retrieval.

5. The Interview Environment

In addition to specifying the content of the diagnostic interview, the environment in which it will be conducted should also be standardized. Standardization of the interview environment increases the efficiency and reduces the potential bias in information retrieval. Thus, interviews should be conducted in similar surroundings from client to client and from social worker to social worker. Where possible, the amount of time given to each interview should be uniform as well as the number of interviews social workers conduct in a day. Other aspects of the interview situation should be routinized whenever possible. These efforts at standardization of the interview environment not only promote efficiency but make possible more valid comparison of the responses of those interviewed, better decisions about resource allocations to different clients and the accumulation of information about groups of comparable clients.

6. Rehearsing the Interview

Before an interview schedule is implemented with agency clients or potential clients, it should be rehearsed by the social workers who will be using it. This can be done by asking colleagues to take the role of a typical respondent presenting a typical problem. During this role-play, the interviewer should practice conveying the purpose of the interview, get familiar with the questions, try various probing techniques, and so on. In a rehearsal, the interviewer can get feedback from the person playing the respondent about ambiguous questions, distracting gestures and habits, and inaccurate reflective statements. The roles can then be reversed. Finally, tape recording mock interviews, listening to and discussing the playback may be additionally instructive.

7. Pretesting the Interview

After the interview has been rehearsed and refined, it should be pretested with two or three applicants for agency service. If possible, and with the applicants' permissions, these interviews should be tape recorded. After completion, the interview tapes are played back to determine whether they provide necessary information, whether they are too long and fatiguing, and whether the interview schedule or interviewer are introducing sources of bias. The interviewer may also ask the respondent questions about issues of time, ambiguity of questions, uncovered topics, and the like.

8. Conducting the Interviews

Once the interview schedule is refined and in final form it is ready to be used in social work practice. Nevertheless, there are certain principles of successful interviewing which must continue to be observed by those using this information-gathering device. Successful interviewing is not simply a matter of reading aloud the words on the page. The interviewer must show an active, concerned interest in what the respondent has to say. In seeking accurate information, and in clarifying responses, the interviewer may need to request validating information through documentation, names of others who may verify information, and so on. In doing so, however, the interviewer should be direct, accepting, and should resist the temptation to play the role of the Grand Inquisitor. In projecting acceptance and nonjudgement, neutral probes should be employed to clarify responses. Here is an example of part of an intake interview in a child abuse agency with a parent suspected of abusing her child.

> Respondent: "Children need to be punished, otherwise they go bad."
>
> Interviewer: "What sorts of punishment do you use when your child is bad?"
>
> Respondent: "Whatever he deserved."
>
> Interviewer: "Can you give me an example of a situation in which he was bad and you gave him punishment?"
>
> Respondent: "I can't remember. Anyway it's my business and not yours."
>
> Interviewer: "I know it's difficult to have a stranger asking you all these personal questions, but for your sake and for your child's, it's important that we get all this information. Your child shows signs of severe beatings from the doctor's reports."
>
> Respondent: "He falls a lot."
>
> Interviewer: "Is there anyone else who we can talk to who can tell us something about that, like a doctor, babysitter, teacher, . . ."

Interviews are also useful tools for generating information about the interviewer's feelings and attitudes. Thus, the content of the interview, the characteristics of the respondents and the interview context can generate powerful emotional responses in the interviewer. Does the respondent provoke anger in the interviewer? Does the interviewer empathize so much with the respondent that unsubstantiated favorable assumptions are made about what the respondent is saying? Only through self-awareness and sensitivity to his/her *own* emotions during and after the interview can this information gathering tool be used fully. This is no simple task when the interviewer is handwriting the responses to questions, attending to the respondent's non-verbal behavior, and is conscious of the time.

9. Recording the Information

In some situations, for example, in semistructured interviews with mostly open-ended questions, it makes sense to tape record responses if that is possible. Structured interviews, on the other hand, with closed-ended questions may employ *self administered* sections to be completed by the respondent. If respondents are well educated, they may be able to give a great deal of straightforward factual information such as name, address, employment status, and so on by filling out a form while waiting to be interviewed. Sometimes, the interview situation is so highly charged, it would be impossible or grossly insensitive for the interviewer to be writing while the respondent is revealing his/her most intimate problems, thoughts, experiences, and the like. In situations such as these, where tape recorders are not used, interviewers should write down relevant information *immediately* after termination of the interview.

Successful interviewing takes hard work, self-awareness and experience. Over time, however, the ability to develop and conduct interviews can be one of the most useful information gathering aids available to the social worker.

HYPOTHETICAL ILLUSTRATION

A small, family service agency which attempts to promote healthy family functioning provides marital counseling and child management services. There are five direct service social workers on staff, one of whom has primary responsibility for intake interviewing. The other four social workers also do intake interviewing, but on a much more limited basis.

This agency, though small, has many referrals for service as well as direct applicants. Line social workers and the agency's administrator would like to manage the intake function more efficiently and generate some statistics about the applicants, their problems, their sources of referral, etc. This information would be useful for future planning. Until now, however, social workers have been each using their own individual interview formats leading to considerable variation in the kind of information gathered. There is a particular need to standardize that portion of the intake interview concerned with marital problems and child management difficulties since these are the agency's primary foci. The task, then, is to develop a standardized interview for assessing applicants' problems in these areas.

1. The Purpose of the Interview

The primary purpose of the interview is to determine the type and severity of the problems experienced by the applicant and whether agency services can help alleviate them. The intake interviewer, on the basis of information gathered, must decide whether the potential client is eligible for agency services or whether s/he should be referred to a private practitioner, a more specialized agency, an agency in another geographic area, and so on.

2. Articulation of the Conceptual Framework and Interview Content

Although the social workers in this agency differ in the kinds of treatment interventions they routinely employ, they do share a problem-focused orientation emphasizing the current situation with which a client is struggling to cope. Since agency clients are voluntary and participate in agency service on a contractual basis, they need to be adequately motivated for treatment to take place and be effective.

The primary intake worker organizes a meeting with the rest of the agency staff in which the categories of information which they all agree are essential for diagnostic, treatment and referral decisions are listed. These categories include applicant identifying information, indications of the range and severity of family problems, descriptions of the conditions which exacerbate these, expressed satisfaction and dissatisfaction with the marriage, level of motivation for treatment, previous involvement in professional counseling, and other sources of help and problem-solving advice.

3 and 4. Constructing the Interview Schedule

Because the social workers in this agency vary in their interviewing styles and treatment approach, a flexible, semistructured interview schedule is chosen. Once the major categories or information dimensions are identified, open and closed-ended questions can be developed. Straightforward, identifying information such as name, age, employment status, and so on may be put in the form of specific, closed-ended questions. Some of these questions may look like the following:

Marital Status
Are you presently married?   Yes ____ No ____
If "yes," for how long have you been married?
    Less than 6 months   ____
    Between 6 months and 1 year   ____
    Between 1 and 2 years   ____
    Between 2 and 5 years   ____
    Between 5 and 10 years   ____
    Between 10 and 15 years   ____
    Over 15 years

Employment Status and Income
Are you currently employed?   Yes ____ No ____
Is your spouse currently employed?   Yes ____ No ____
What is your combined annual income?
    Less than $6,000 per year   ____
    Between 6,000 and 7,999   ____
    Between 8,000 and 9,999   ____
    Between 10,000 and 14,999   ____
    Between 15,000 and 19,999   ____
    Between 20,000 and 24,999   ____
    Over 25,000   ____

More discursive questions need to be asked in an open-ended format. Some of these questions might look like the following:

Reasons for request for service

Why did you come to this agency?

What do you see as your major family or marital problems?

When did these problems start?

Has anything happened recently to make them worse and to lead you to seek outside help?

What kind of help would you like to receive?

Having specified examples of questions within each important information category, the person constructing the schedule should organize the categories and questions in a logical order, eliminating question-overlap or redundancy, eliminating overlap or gaps in answer categories in forced-choice questions, and so on. An introductory statement should be devised which informs the applicant of the purpose of the interview, assures the applicant of confidentiality, and indicates how the information collected will be used. Instructions for the interviewers with regard to probing and clarifying interview responses and gathering necessary documentation also should be developed. Next, the schedule should be put together, making sure it is legible and uncluttered and that open-ended questions have sufficient space provided after them for the intake worker to record full and complete responses to them. Finally, a closing statement should be composed.

5. Standardization of The Interview Environment

Some decisions then need to be made regarding the interview environment. Should the couple be interviewed together or separately? How long should each interview take? Where should the interviews take place? What style of address, demeanor, clothing are appropriate to the agency and interview context?

6. Rehearsing the Interview

Once the foregoing questions are answered, the interview should be rehearsed among staff with staff alternating in the roles of applicant and interviewer. Various types of applicants such as husband, wife, recalcitrant, nervous, hostile, and depressed applicants are role-played. Probes and clarifying questions are practiced. These simulations should be tape recorded. The playbacks are then discussed among workers so that necessary changes can be made in the interview schedules and in individual interviewer behavior.

7. Pretesting the Interview Schedule

The interview schedule is then tried out with one or two service applicants, asking their permission to tape record the interview and explaining why. After the formal interview is completed, respondents are asked to indicate whether they felt that any important questions had been left out and/or whether any questions seemed unnecessary or repetitious. The tape recordings are then reviewed, and further changes in the schedule are made.

8. Conducting the Interviews

The new interview schedule is now ready for routine implementation with agency applicants. Efforts are made by the primary intake worker and other social workers who occasionally do intake to use the schedule in a standardized manner. Any problems which seem to arise in a number of interviews should be discussed so that necessary modification in the interview schedule can be considered.

9. Recording the Information

When a reasonable number of interviews have been completed, interview protocols should be reviewed to see whether information is fully and legibly recorded, whether all interviewers are asking all relevant questions and whether necessary supporting information and documentation is gathered. Final revision in the interview schedule or instructions to interviewers may take place at this point.

EXERCISE

Identify a major function of a unit of a social work agency in which you are currently working. For that function, identify the information that needs to be gathered for diagnostic decisions to be made. Devise a questionnaire to elicit that information from program applicants or clients. Compare your questionnaire with the devices currently employed to gather this information. How does your procedure compare with existing agency procedures?

SELECTED BIBLIOGRAPHY

Epstein, Irwin and Tony Tripodi, *Research Techniques for Program Planning, Monitoring, and Evaluation* (New York: Columbia University Press, 1977), pp. 20–28.

Fear, Richard A., *The Evaluation Interview* (2d ed.; New York: McGraw-Hill, 1973), pp. 14–41.

Fellin, Phillip, "The Standardized Interview in Social Work Research," *Social Casework* (February 1963) 44(2):81–85.

Goldstein, Harris K., *Research Standards and Methods for Social Workers,* (New Orleans: Hauser Press, 1963), pp. 143–48.

Gottman, John M. and Sandra R. Leiblum, *How To Do Psychotherapy and How To Evaluate It* (New York: Holt, Rinehart and Winston, 1974), pp. 33–38.

Jenkins, Shirley, "Collecting Data by Questionnaire and Interview," in Norman A. Polansky, ed., *Social Work Research* (rev. ed.; Chicago: University of Chicago Press, 1975), pp. 131–53.

Kadushin, Alfred, *The Social Work Interview* (New York: Columbia University Press, 1972), pp. 1–218.

Meyer, Victor, Andrée Liddell, and Maureen Lyons, "Behavioral Interviews," in Anthony Ciminero, Karen S. Calhoun, and Harry E. Adams, eds., *Handbook of Behavioral Assessment* (New York: Wiley, 1977), pp. 117–52.

Moser, C. A., *Survey Methods in Social Investigation* (London: Heinemann Educational Books, 1957), pp. 185–209.

Payne, Stanley L., *The Art of Asking Questions* (Princeton, N.J.: Princeton University Press, 1951), pp. 228–37.

3

USING AVAILABLE INSTRUMENTS

Some applied research problems require the development of wholly original research instruments such as interview schedules or questionnaires. Others do not. In the latter cases, existing research instruments can be used directly or modified slightly to suit the unique features of the context to which they will be applied. Consequently, to employ research tools in their practice, clinical social workers need not invent new information-gathering devices every time they wish to collect valid and reliable information. Indeed, they should first determine whether suitable instruments already exist before launching into the development of original ones.

Existing instruments appear in many guises. There are standardized questionnaires, statistical forms, observation guides, rating scales, draw-a-picture tests, interpret-a-picture tests, and so on. These data-gathering devices and their uses are described in published literature and, occasionally, in agency reports. If they are in copywrit, the copyright holders's permission must be secured to use them. If not, permission is not required. Some instruments, of course, require considerable training to be properly used. We do not recommend their use by the untrained. Thus, for example, we are not suggesting that clinical social workers without proper training routinely incorporate Rorschach or Thematic Apperception Tests (TAT's) into their diagnostic interviews. However, many other existing instruments can be obtained and applied easily, by clinical social workers, without extensive training. In this chapter, we offer some guidelines for locating, selecting and applying available research instruments to diagnostic assessment.

THE CLINICAL USE OF AVAILABLE INSTRUMENTS

As we suggested earlier, existing research instruments can be used directly, that is, in their original form. Or, they can be used indirectly and modified, revised or adapted to the unique requirements of a new research/practice situation. For diagnostic assessment, available instruments can be used in the following ways:

1. They can generate information directly relevant to diagnostic assessment. Thus, for example, problem checklists already in use in community mental health settings may be applied to other comparable settings or contexts in which client self-assessments of problems are required.
2. They can generate discussion which is relevant to diagnostic assessment. Thus, a TAT card, depicting a conflict between an adult male and an adult female, may be used to generate discussion between a husband and wife in the initial stages of conjoint therapy. This discussion can be a source of critical information about the types of conflicts the couple is having and how they go about trying to resolve them.
3. They can provide information about how a potential client compares with a normative population which has already been tested with the instrument. Thus, standardized reading tests can provide information about how a child who is referred to a school social worker compares with his/her age-mates in this mode of academic performance.
4. They can serve as a starting point for the development of an original research instrument. Thus, for example, an existing instrument may provide ideas about issues to be covered, question format, response systems, and so on, which when

properly modified can be used for generating information relevant to problem assessment.

Available instruments are applicable also to treatment monitoring and evaluation. In monitoring a client's compliance with a group treatment contract, for example, an existing group observation instrument can be used to monitor the character of a client's participation in group therapy sessions and how often s/he actively participates.

Perhaps the most frequent use of available instruments, however, is in gathering data to measure the extent to which client and social worker objectives have been realized as a result of social work intervention. This evaluative use of available instruments is exemplified in the widespread utilization of techniques such as goal-attainment scaling in community mental health settings. These instruments generate detailed information about treatment efficacy.

Although this chapter presents a set of principles for locating, selecting and utilizing existing research instruments for diagnostic assessment, the foregoing treatment, monitoring and evaluative uses should also be kept in mind. In other words, the following principles are equally applicable to locating, selecting and utilizing existing research instruments for diagnostic assessment, treatment monitoring and evaluation.

PRINCIPLES FOR USING AVAILABLE INSTRUMENTS

1. The Purpose of the Instrument

In considering the use of an existing research instrument, one should first specify its purpose. Is it intended for diagnostic, treatment monitoring or evaluative purposes? Thus, one should determine at which stage in the clinical process the instrument is to be used.

Another important question involves the type of knowledge, information or data which best suits this purpose. Should the information take the form of quantitative data, qualitative data or hypotheses? *Quantitative data* puts information into numerical form. Questions about the frequency of drug use, incidents of depression, marital conflicts, and the like, yield quantitative information. *Qualitative data* offers information in narrative form. Thus, asking applicants to describe their feelings concerning divorce, death, marriage, career, and so on, will generally yield rich narrative or qualitative responses. Open-ended response systems encourage such responses. Finally, information may be presented in the form of hypotheses. *Hypotheses* are statements about possible *cause-effect relationships*. Some research instruments, for example, are suited to generating hypotheses about the causes of client problems. Asking applicants to describe their life circumstances when they began drinking might generate *causal hypotheses* about possible causes of a drinking problem. At the very least, such questions will generate *correlational hypotheses* about which problems seem to occur at the same time. Thus, asking the applicant whether incidents of spouse abuse are likely to take place during drinking bouts may yield a correlational hypothesis about the correlates or concomitants of the applicant's drinking behavior.

The more specific one can be about the purpose for which an instrument is to be used, and the kind of information which is required of it, the more efficient will be the search for it.

2. *Locating and Assessing Available Instruments*

How does one locate relevant, available research instruments? Here are some suggestions:

a. In some forms of therapy or intervention, research instruments are routinely employed. Thus, for example, behavioral assessment instruments are used by behavioral therapists, psychological tests by clinical psychologists, and so on. Asking colleagues who use such instruments as a standard part of their practice is one way to locate relevant instruments.

b. Relevant instruments also may be located in the professional literature devoted to the kinds of problems or forms of intervention in which the social worker is interested. Basic practice journals such as *Social Work, Social Casework, Behavior Therapy,* and the like, frequently publish articles describing research instruments. Problem-focused journals such as the *Journal of Alcoholism and Drug Abuse, The Journal of Crime and Delinquency, Probation,* and the like, publish descriptions and critiques of such instruments as well. If the instruments are not fully described, or if the author's permission is necessary to use the instrument, these journals generally indicate the author's institutional affiliation and address.

c. Locating all relevant articles is another matter. There are, however, published guides to the research literature that cite studies by subject or by the key concepts with which they are concerned—for example, *The Reader's Guide to Periodical Literature, Psychology Abstracts, Sociology Abstracts, Social Work Abstracts, Poverty and Human Resources Abstracts.* The abstract journals publish a brief description of each article cited. Finally, the subject index of the card catalogue of a good research library, say in a nearby school of social work, can be used for this purpose.

d. Probably the most efficient way to locate instruments as well as critical reviews of them is by using resources such as the following collections of research instruments:

Charles M. Bonjean, Richard J. Hill, and S. Dale Mclemore, *Sociological Measurement: An Inventory of Scales and Indices* (San Francisco: Chandler, 1967).

Oscar K. Buros, *Personality Tests and Reviews II* (Highland Park, N.J.: Gryphon Press, 1975).

Oscar K. Buros, *The Seventh Mental Measurements Yearbook* (Highland Park, N.J.: Gryphon Press, 1972).

Orval G. Johnson and James Rommarito, *Tests and Measurements in Child Development: A Handbook* (San Francisco: Jossey-Bass, 1971).

Dale G. Lake, Matthew B. Miles, and Ralph Earle, Jr., eds., *Measuring Human Behavior* (New York and London: Teachers College Press, Columbia University, 1973).

John P. Robinson and Phillip R. Shaver, *Measures of Social Psychological Attitudes* (Ann Arbor: University of Michigan, Institute for Social Research, 1969).

Anita Simon and E. Gil Boyer, *Mirrors for Behavior: An Anthology of Classroom Observation Instruments* (Philadelphia: Research for Better Schools, 1971).

Murray A. Strauss, *Family Measurement Techniques* (Minneapolis: University of Minnesota Press, 1969).

e. Finally, research institutes, research centers and research departments within social agencies often describe research instruments in their publications and reports of research projects. These organizations and organizational units may be located within universities such as the University of Michigan's Institute for Social Research or within private and governmental agencies such as the Child Welfare League of America and the National Institute of Mental Health.

3. Determining the Relevance of Available Instruments

In the context of diagnostic assessment, one should seek instruments that provide information pertinent to diagnostic decision-making. In addition, the information generated by the instrument should be consistent with the intervention techniques and treatment goals endorsed by the agency. Equally important, the instrument should be appropriate to the clientele of the agency. Rorschach Tests are not applicable to the blind. Self-administered questionnaires are unapplicable to illiterates. And so on. No matter how reliable and valid the instrument, it is only relevant if it facilitates diagnostic assessment by the social worker.

4. Looking for Built-In Bias

Closely related to the issue of relevance is the question of whether existing instruments contain any built-in biases which might distort assessments of certain classes of respondents. Thus, some instruments have been shown to favor some classes of individuals at the expense of others. It has been asserted, for example, that I.Q. tests are biased in favor of urban, middle-class, white males. Marital conflict assessment tests standardized with middle-class respondents may lead to incorrect judgments of "deep pathology" when applied to working-class families. What is "pathological" in one social grouping may be normative in another. While there is no ironclad rule for determining whether such bias exists in an instrument, some effort should be made to look over the instrument for obvious bias, to determine the social characteristics of the groups on which the instrument was developed and tested, and finally, to read the published critiques of the instrument. Interpretations based on built-in biases can lead to serious errors in clinical judgment.

5. Determining the Reliability of Available Instruments

An instrument is reliable if it produces the same results with repeated trials on the same basic information. Thus, for example, a reliable rating scale for measuring the level of physical impairment of a disabled person will produce the same rating, when applied repeatedly, to the same disabled person, assuming that there have been no changes in his/her actual level of disability.

Researchers commonly assess instrument reliability in four ways: *test-retest*, *inter-observer*, *parallel-instrument*, and *split-half* reliability. Test-retest reliability is assessed by taking repeated measurements on the same dimension or variable—for example, the level of patient anxiety prior to psychotherapy—over time. Assuming that the anxiety level has remained relatively constant (usually measures are taken within a short space of time to support this assumption), a reliable instrument would produce consistent anxiety ratings. Test-retest reliability is often reported in the form of a statistic called a *correlation coefficient*. Correlation coefficients used to measure reliability generally vary in strength from 0.00 to 1.00. A test-retest reliability coefficient of 0.00 represents complete nonreliability, 0.50, only moderate reliability, 0.70 high reliability, and 1.00 perfect reliability. Occasionally, when a single observer is rating a phenomenon, test-retest reliability is referred to as *intra-observer* or *intra-rater* reliability. Irrespective of the label applied, it is a measure of the "stability" of the instrument over time.

When more than one observer rates a phenomenon—for example, when caseworkers rate the level of motivation for treatment from the same case record—*inter-observer* or *inter-rater* reliability refers to the extent to which different caseworkers will give the same case record the same motivation for treatment score. Measures of inter-observer reliability are often expressed in correlational terms (as above) or in terms of percentage agreement. When the latter is used, 70 percent agreement or more indicates a reasonably high level of inter-observer reliability.

A third approach to assessing the reliability of research instruments involved correlating the results of "parallel" measures of the same phenomenon. Say, for example, we are interested in utilizing available measures of school adjustment. The latter concept would include variables such as academic grades and classroom conduct. To assess the reliability of these as parallel measures of school adjustment, one would look at the correlations between each of these dimensions, that is, grades and conduct. In doing so, a researcher would employ correlation coefficients (for example, Pearson's *r*, Spearman's rho) which describe relationships in positive or negative terms. These measures range from -1.00 to $+1.00$ and indicate the *direction* as well as the strength of the relationship between measures. A negative correlation would indicate an *inverse* relationship between grades and classroom conduct. This finding would suggest that the measures have a low degree of "equivalence" and that one or both were unreliable measures of school adjustment. A correlation around 0.00 would indicate no relationship between grades and classroom conduct and would again suggest that at least one of the measures was unreliable. A positive correlation would indicate a *direct* relationship between grades and classroom conduct. However, in order to justify the assumption that each of these measures was a reliable measure of school adjustment one would expect a positive correlation of $+.50$ or better. Only such a positive correlation would indicate that the two measures were equivalent or parallel measures of school adjustment.

Split-half reliability is based on logic similar to the preceding approach. The difference is that split-half reliability assesses a single measure. In this form of reliability testing an attempt is made to judge the internal consistency of the component parts of a single measure. Say, for example, a ten question instrument purported to measure marital compatibility. To test the split-half reliability of this instrument, the ten questions would be randomly assigned to two groups of five questions apiece. The cumulative scores on these two groups are then correlated. A high positive correlation (+.70 or better) would indicate a high internal consistency among the component questions of the instrument.

The foregoing modes of reliability testing get at different aspects of instrument reliability. The tests used should fit the research situation. If only one rater is used, inter-rater reliability should be assessed. If more than one is used, inter-rater reliability is appropriate. If more than one measure is used parallel instrument reliability should be determined. If a single instrument with many component questions is used, split-half reliability is in order. Finally, if one intends to use an instrument to measure change or stability over time, test-retest reliability is essential.

Overall, in contemplating the use of available instruments, it is important to determine whether previous uses of the instrument indicate a high level of appropriate reliability. If they do not, or if no reliability tests are reported, one should be very cautious about employing the instrument without first doing one's own reliability testing. Even if such reliability reports do exist, if time and resources allow, it is a good idea to do one's own testing. This would insure the fact that there is nothing different about the way the instrument is administered or the population on whom it is administered that would reduce the reliability of the instrument. Unfortunately, however, this kind of thoroughness can rarely be afforded in practice contexts.

6. Determining the Validity of Available Instruments

An instrument is valid if it measures what it claims to measure. From a purely logical standpoint, validity concerns itself with the extent to which the measurement device is directly relevant to the concept being measured. Researchers refer to this as *face validity* or *content validity.* Thus, an instrument intended to measure whether a couple would be suitable as adoptive parents that did not have questions about their attitudes toward children would have low face validity.

Predictive validity refers to whether the measure predicts other phenomena that are assumed to be associated with the variable being measured. Using the previous example, the instrument would have high predictive validity if those couples who scored high on the "suitability index" were more likely to complete the application process, were more likely to receive adoptive placements and, most important, made better adoptive parents than those who scored low in suitability. These relationships are expressed in the form of correlation coefficients.

Sometimes it is impossible to wait long enough to test the predictive validity of an instrument. In such instances, researchers assess validity empirically by correlating the instrument with other measures which are presumed to measure the same variable. This is referred to a *concurrent validity.* Considering our potential adoptive parents again, one might correlate their suitability as measured by their expressed attitudes about children with an observational instrument which assesses the manner in which they relate to children currently in their home.

Closely related to concurrent validity is *construct validity.* When a measure has high construct validity, it is highly correlated with other measures that are hypothetically related to the variable to be measured, but are not attempting to measure the same thing. Thus, one would assume that high suitability scores would be associated with psychological tests designed to measure emotional maturity.

Ideally, all research instruments should be validated in all of the above mentioned ways. Typically, however, authors simply discuss content validity or the logical fit between the instrument and what it is intended to measure. When correlation coefficients are reported, as in predictive, concurrent or construct validity, these correlations are likely to be weaker than those reported in tests of reliability. In the context of validity, then, correlations of +.30 to +.50 would be high enough to warrant the cautious use of the instrument. When correlation coefficients are not reported, the reader should him/herself assess the fit between the concept to be measured and the instrument used to measure it. Are they logically related? Are there significant components of the variable to be measured which are left out of the index? These are critical questions to ask before utilizing an available instrument.

7. Determining the Availability of Test Norms

Along with reliability and validity estimates, the user of an available research instrument should ascertain a description of the population or populations with whom the instrument was tested and standardized. An instrument which was developed and first used in an urban context may be inappropriate for use in a rural community. Tests developed with one class or subcultural group will not be valid and reliable with another.

Some tests, have been so widely used and broadly standardized that *test norms* have been established for comparing individual respondents to a larger population in order to make judgments about the individual's relative performance. This is particularly true for academic performance tests conducted in the schools. These statistical norms are invaluable in assessing a child's or a group of children's relative performance as compared with their age-mates.

When test norms are not available, at the very least, one should attempt to find out the social characteristics of those who were subjects in the original development of the instrument. How similar are they to the population with whom they are intended to be used?

8. Determining the Adequacy of Knowledge Generated by Available Instruments

As we indicated earlier, available instruments can aid diagnostic assessment in numerous ways. Specifically, they can: (1) generate information directly relevant to diagnostic assessment; (2) generate discussion with the service applicant, which, in turn, can serve as a basis for diagnostic assessment; (3) generate information about how a potential client compares with a normative population; and (4) serve as a starting point for the generation of an original research instrument.

Once the purpose, relevance, sources of bias, reliability, validity, and normative bases of an instrument have been assessed, it is possible for the clinical social worker to judge the adequacy of the information generated by the instrument relative to his/her intended purpose. An instrument which is desired for use as a direct diagnostic tool for a large pool of potential clients, over a period of time should demonstrate relatively high degrees of content validity, test-retest reliability, and be standardized on a population similar to the population of service applicants. If individual applicant scores are to be compared with scores derived from a normative population, it is absolutely essential that the population of applicants be comparable to the population with whom the instrument was standardized. Any dissimilarities are likely to be exaggerated with a clinical population and can lead to useless, misleading and even harmful generalization from test results.

Alternatively, if available instruments are to serve as stimuli for discussion, or for instrument generation, issues of reliability and standardization are less important. Instrument relevance and content validity, however, remain as important dimensions for instrument assessment.

9. Determining the Feasibility of Using Available Instruments

Having assessed the extent to which an instrument is likely to satisfy knowledge requirements, a final consideration is its feasibility. This refers to the practical factors involved in an instrument's use. Among these factors are the following: cost, time, respondent requirements, and staff training requirements.

Financial costs include the cost of purchasing and administering an instrument as well as the indirect costs associated with taking staff away from other agency activities. In general, standardized test forms are more expensive than non-standardized instruments but they yield more reliable results. In addition, one must consider the direct and indirect costs of analyzing and interpreting the information generated by the instrument in assessing its feasibility.

A second set of considerations is the time involved in administering, analyzing, and interpreting the information. Generally speaking, more frequent administration of an instrument is likely to provide more reliable information. Frequent administration also costs more money and time. More than likely, a balance is struck between the time and cost factors on the one hand, and the need for reliability on the other. Alternative sources of new information as well as validating information also should be considered as a way of keeping costs down.

Some instruments, particularly self-administered questionnaires, require a relatively high degree of literacy and sophistication on the part of respondents. Here the fit between the characteristics of those who are likely to be respondents and the requirements of competent instrument completion must be considered. Many an illiterate or only partially literate respondent has completed a self-administered questionnaire rather than admit to his/her reading problem. The result is a complete but meaningless set of information. This issue comes up as well when respondents are not fluent in the language in which the questionnaire is written.

Finally, one should consider the knowledge requirements associated with administering and interpreting the instrument. Some instruments such as TAT and Rorschach tests require a great deal of training and experience for them to be administered and interpreted competently. These instruments should be used by qualified experts only. Many other available instruments, however, are not difficult to understand and to employ. When these instruments serve the clinician's purpose, function within the ethical and value constraints of his/her profession and are acceptable and understandable to the service applicant, they can greatly facilitate diagnostic decision-making.

HYPOTHETICAL ILLUSTRATION

A clinician employed by the student counseling division of a university spends most of his/her time working with young adults who are having difficulties with interpersonal adjustment. Basing much of his/her diagnostic decision-making on role-theory, s/he is interested in developing an efficient and systematic procedure for assessing relationships between service applicants and "significant others" in their environment.

1. The Purpose of the Instrument

The purpose of the instrument is to assess interpersonal relationships with significant others in the applicant's environment. The social worker is interested as well in finding an instrument which is compatible with role theory, but does not require a high level of specialized training or expertise for its administration.

2. Locating and Assessing an Instrument

Looking through Lake's et al. *Measuring Human Behavior*, s/he comes across the Role Construct Repertory Test devised by Kelly, which appears to be potentially useful. On reading further, however, s/he discovers that the instrument should be used only by therapists expert in Kelly's theory of role constructs. Since the social worker has neither the time nor inclination to develop this expertise, that option is impractical. On still further reading, the social worker discovers that there are references to simpler versions of the test with citations to research by Bieri et al. (1970) on the concept of "cognitive complexity." Although the concept is unfamiliar, the work cited offers a straightforward explanation of the concept and a modified and simplified version of Kelly's original instrument. The new instrument, known as the Rep Test, is clearly described. It has respondents rating themselves as well as significant others such as friends of both sexes, each parent, and other role-types along various personality dimensions such as decisiveness, shyness, dependency, maladjustment, and so on. Although simple and efficient in its administration, the instrument provides considerable information about how the respondent sees him/herself and significant others in his/her environment.

3. Determining the Relevance of the Instruments

The instrument, in its modified form, is highly relevant to the social worker's purpose. It deals with many of the roles and personality dimensions which are salient to counseling young college students. Role types are not exhaustive, however, and consideration is given to adding the role of professor and roommate to it. In addition, the inclusion of certain personality dimensions such as assertiveness is considered. Irrespective of these possible modifications, the instrument is judged to be directly relevant to the social worker's theoretical perspective and to the information which is desired.

4. Looking for Built-In Bias

Although the modified instrument is highly relevant to the clinician's needs, it is clear that two major sources of "bias" will emerge from total reliance on it. First, the instrument is based on the applicant's self ratings of him/herself and those in the environment. Relying totally on these perceptions leaves the clinician vulnerable to systematic distortions which may characterize the applicant's world view. Moreover, the personality ratings are not behaviorally specific. What is extreme shyness to one respondent may be quite normal to another. Such disagreements may also exist between social workers and their clients. Finally, different social workers may disagree about these dimensions.

Recognizing these sources of potential bias, it would be important for the social worker to gather additional information based on his/her observations of the applicant, the observations of significant others if possible, and so on, to validate the applicant's account of him/herself and those in the environment. In addition, the social worker may wish to gather more behaviorally specific information about the bases upon which the applicant is judging him/herself or others as shy, dependent, assertive, and the like. This validation of the applicant's perceptions would be necessary for sound diagnostic decision-making.

5. Determining the Reliability of the Instrument

Although published discussions of the Rep Test report no tests of how it correlates with other parallel instruments, tests of test-retest reliability are reported. Thus, Tripodi and Bieri (1966) report a test-retest correlation of $+.70$ indicating relatively high reliability on that basis.

6. Determining the Validity of the Instrument

The instrument appears to have a high level of face or content validity as well as test-retest reliability. Thus, it directly attends to the role types and personality dimensions which are salient to the social worker as well as to the potential client population. In fact, the instrument was primarily developed and tested on a population of college students. This form of validity is based, however, on the judgment of the social worker rather than on any statistical tests.

As far as statistical measures of validity are concerned, there is some evidence that the scores on the test are predictive of cognitive complexity and attitude change. While this relationship is not extremely high ($r = .35$), it is a reasonable indicator of predictive validity. It is clear, however, that there is no statistical evidence of concurrent or predictive validity in relation to what the instrument itself is intended to measure. This is another reason why the social worker should validate the perceptions of applicants with additional information before making diagnostic decisions.

7. Determining the Availability of Test Norms

The test was developed and used with college student populations primarily, however, no test norms are currently available. Hence, no judgments can be made about how individual applicants compare with nonclinical populations of college students.

8. Determining the Adequacy of Knowledge Generated by the Instrument

Although the instrument is not an exhaustive nor a definitive diagnostic instrument, the knowledge it produces can facilitate diagnostic decision-making in a number of ways. First, it can provide direct information about how the applicant sees him/herself and significant others in his/her environment. Second, self and other ratings on the instrument can generate useful discussion with the applicant regarding his/her perceptions of self and others. This discussion may lead to possible judgments about the applicant's level of insight and his/her capacity for treatment as well. Third, the instrument can serve as a starting point for the development of a new instrument which is more finely attuned to the requirements of the social worker's task and setting. Finally, though no test norms are available, the instrument can be used to compare subpopulations of students applying to the clinic for counseling. Thus, male students can be compared to females, minorities to nonminorities, and so on. Such comparisons can provide important implications for planning, policy development, and staff training programs.

9. Determining the Feasibility of Using the Instrument

Since the instrument takes from fifteen minutes to one half hour to complete, is self-administered, and is relatively easy for college students to reliably complete, implementation is quite feasible. In fact, it would be possible to include the instrument in a self-administered informational questionnaire given to students prior to the first assessment interview. The intake worker could then use the applicant's self and other ratings for a deeper and more productive first interview.

Exercise

Locate two instruments that can be used to assess marital adjustment problems. Evaluate each instrument in terms of the dimensions discussed in this chapter. Compare their relative advantages and disadvantages in relation to your practice orientation and the setting in which you work.

SELECTED BIBLIOGRAPHY

Arkava, Morton L. and Mark Snow, *Psychological Tests and Social Work Practice* (Springfield, Ill.: Charles C. Thomas, 1978), pp. 1–48 and 87–89.

Anastasi, Anne, *Psychological Testing* (3d ed.; New York: 1968), pp. 3–157 and 627–50.

Bieri, James, Alvin L. Atkins, Scott Briar, Robin Lobeck, Henry Miller, and Tony Tripodi, "The Nature of Cognitive Structures" in Peter B. Warr, ed., *Thought and Personality* (Harmondsworth, Eng.: Penguin, 1970), pp. 160–77.

Ciminero, Anthony R., Karen S. Calhoun, and Henry E. Adams, eds., *Handbook of Behavioral Assessment* (New York: Wiley, 1977), pp. 79–113, and 153–94.

Cronback, Lee J., *Essentials of Psychological Testing* (2d ed.; New York: Harper, 1960), p. 148.

Fitzpatrick, Robert, "The Selection of Measures for Evaluating Programs," in *Evaluative Research*, Seminar on Evaluative Research, American Institutes for Research, Pittsburgh, January 1970, pp. 67–82.

Gottman John M. and Sandra R. Leiblum, *How To Do Psychotherapy and How To Evaluate It* (New York: Holt, Rinehart and Winston), pp. 29–33.

Lake, Dale G., Matthew B. Miles, and Ralph B. Earle, Jr., eds., *Measuring Human Behavior: Tools for the Assessment of Social Functioning* (New York: Teacher College Press, Columbia University, 1973), p. 341.

Liberman, Robert P., William J. DeRisi, Larry W. King, Thad A. Eckman, and David Wort, "Behavioral Measurement in a Community Mental Health Center," in Park O. Davison, Frank W. Clark, and Lee A. Hamerlynck, eds., *Evaluation of Behavioral Programs* (Champaign, Ill.: Research Press, 1974), pp. 103–40.

Schnerger, James M. and David G. Watterson, "Using Tests and Other Information in Counseling," Institute for Personality and Ability Testing, Champaign, Ill., 1977, pp. 89–138.

Thomas, Edwin J., "Uses of Research Methods in Interpersonal Practice," in Norman A. Polansky, ed., *Social Work Research* (rev. ed.; Chicago: University of Chicago Press, 1975), pp. 258–64.

Tripodi, Tony, *Uses and Abuses of Social Research in Social Work* (New York: Columbia University Press, 1974), pp. 113–36.

Tripodi, Tony and James Bieri, "Cognitive Complexity, Perceived Conflict, and Certainty," *Journal of Personality* (March 1966), 34(1):144–53.

Wolman, Benjamin B., ed., *Handbook of Clinical Psychology* (New York: McGraw-Hill, 1965), pp. 451–620.

4

SYSTEMATIC OBSERVATION

Direct observation is probably the most natural method of gathering information. All of us observe phenomena continually and make decisions based upon our observations. Similarly, in their practice, clinical social workers routinely observe their clients and base diagnostic and treatment decisions upon what their clients say and do. In the context of social research, however, observation is conducted more systematically than in daily life or in much of clinical practice.

In its most structured form, *systematic observation* is a method of quantitative data collection that involves one or more observers, observing events or behaviors as they occur, and reliably recording their observations in terms of previously structured numerical categories. In some observational studies, the events or behaviors to be observed are first preserved on film, videotape, or audiotape recordings. Observations may take place through one-way mirrors as well. Whatever the means of access to the observational data, systematic observation is sufficiently structured to allow testing of research hypotheses.

At the other end of the observational research continuum, unstructured or *nonsystematic observation* involves one or more observers recording narrative or qualitative accounts of their observations without employing previously structured numerical categories for describing events or behaviors. In social research, it is used to generate research hypotheses. Clinical social workers, however, engage in this form of qualitative observation all the time. Their training and practice experience enables them to make highly refined use of these observations for diagnostic and treatment purposes. To this store of knowledge, we have nothing to add. Instead, this chapter focuses on systematic observation, a procedure which is not typically included in social work education, but one which we think can contribute to diagnostic and treatment decision-making.

More specifically, we concentrate on the use of systematic observation to study *individuals* interacting in families, groups, and in other social institutions. Our intent is to provide clinical social workers with systematic observational principles and techniques that can assist in diagnostic assessments of these individuals. For those readers interested in group assessment techniques, however, we recommend Rosen and Polansky's (1975) excellent article referred to in the selected bibliography at the end of the chapter.

SYSTEMATIC OBSERVATION AND CLINICAL SOCIAL WORK

In social research, observational techniques are frequently resorted to when other, more obtrusive approaches such as self-administered questionnaires or interviews are impractical. For instance, in situations in which research subjects are biased, unable to recall events, hostile, uninterested, or untrained in the concepts with which the researcher is concerned, systematic observational techniques are most useful. Likewise, clinical social workers can employ systematic observation to generate practice relevant information, in natural settings, with persons who for one reason or another cannot be relied upon to make accurate assessments of their own behavior. Thus, systematic observational techniques can be valuable diagnostic tools in schools, mental hospitals, institutions for the retarded, and so on.

Systematic observational techniques are potentially useful in all phases of clinical social work practice. In diagnostic assessment, for example, observations of individuals referred for treatment can be made by social workers, other professionals, or significant others in the referred individual's environment. The contents of these observations can include both the problems and the strengths that the individual brings to social situations. For instance, observational techniques can be used to assess the frequency of provocative behavior within the family, disruptive classroom behaviors, or physically self-destructive behaviors in an institutional setting. Alternatively, these techniques can supply information about positive expressions of affection in a family, cooperative behavior in the classroom, and self-caring behaviors in an institutional setting.

Systematic observation also can be employed to validate information obtained by other, less rigorous procedures. For example, a mother may bring her child to a child-guidance clinic for social work help. A discussion with the mother reveals that she is troubled by her child's "immature behavior." The mother is unable to be very specific, however, about the nature of these behaviors or their frequency. In addition, it is unclear whether these behaviors are "abnormal" in frequency and kind when compared to the behaviors of other children of the same age. By visiting the home, and using systematic observation, the social worker can better assess the specific nature of the behaviors which are problematic to the mother and their frequency. Moreover, s/he can observe the mother's efforts to reduce the occurrence of these behaviors. In this way, the social worker can determine whether the "problem" is with the child or with the mother's expectations.

Systematic observation can be used as well to monitor the extent to which clients follow treatment plans. In fact, the monitoring can be done by clients themselves. Thus, for example, a husband and wife may be instructed to follow a relaxation procedure for five minutes before every evening meal. The objective of this is to reduce tension and angry outbursts during dinner. Both husband and wife may be asked to record on a simple form the number of times during the week that they followed this procedure as well as the number of arguments that they had during dinner. Such systematic recording will give the social worker an indication of the extent to which the clients are complying with treatment procedures and whether these procedures are having any positive effect.

Finally, systematic observation can be employed to evaluate the effectiveness of treatment. This would require recording problematic behaviors or mood states before, during, and after treatment to determine whether they have declined significantly and whether the benefits of treatment persist even after treatment has been terminated. For example, a parent of an overly dependent eight-year-old child currently in therapy may be asked to record the number of times per week the child plays with neighborhood children. This recording is maintained for awhile after treatment ends to determine whether treatment gains persist. If they do not, treatment may resume as before, or the social worker may consider whether or not the child's mother is subverting his/her new-found independence in any way.

PRINCIPLES OF SYSTEMATIC OBSERVATION

1. Determining What Is To Be Observed

To observe a phenomenon reliably, one must decide upon the behaviors to include and to exclude from systematic observation. It is impossible to observe and record everything. Consequently, one should decide on the purpose of the observation before considering techniques of observation. In the context of clinical social work practice, observation-generated information should assist the social worker in carrying out practice-related tasks. In the assessment phase of practice, the information should be linked to diagnostic decision-making.

The contents of observational data may be either public or private (Howe 1976). *Public* observation involves behaviors that are directly discernible to others, e.g., crying, laughing, hitting, and the like. *Private* observation involves self-reported moods or feeling states such as despair, sense of well-being, and feelings of anger. Private observations are directly observable to those experiencing the feeling states, but indirectly observable to those around them. As a result, systematic observation is generally confined to observation of public behaviors. Since more than one observer can observe the same set of public behaviors, higher reliability can be achieved. For those instances in which self-reports or private moods and feeling states are required, we will discuss the use of self-reports and measurement scales in subsequent chapters.

2. *Assessing the Availability of Existing Observational Instruments*

Referring to the principles for assessing available instruments presented in the previous chapter, one should determine whether instruments exist which can be used directly or which can serve as stimuli for the construction of new observational devices.

Some examples of existing observational instruments are available in the selected bibliography at the end of this chapter. These include, Bales Interaction Process Analysis (Bales 1970), the Behavioral Observation Instrument (Liberman et al. 1974), and an instrument for observing living environments (Cataldo and Risley 1974). Bales Interaction Process Analysis is a procedure for classifying verbal behaviors of group participants. After training in this method, observers can reliably classify group members' behaviors in terms of the extent to which they show agreement, solidarity, tension release, disagreement, antagonism, and so on. The Behavioral Observation Instrument, on the other hand, is used to classify the behaviors of individual psychiatric patients in clinical settings such as mental hospital wards. Frequently, attending staff are trained in this method to systematically observe how and where patients spend their time. Behaviors such as walking, talking, smoking, and sitting are recorded with this method. Finally, the Cataldo and Risley device can be used to observe children or retarded adults in institutional settings based on their use of play materials and their interactions with other residents. If appropriate observational instruments do not already exist, an original instrument can be devised using the following principles.

3. Constructing the Observational Instrument

The basic task in constructing observation instruments is to provide well-defined, easy to understand dimensions and categories that can be reliably and accurately recorded. Attached to the instrument should be a set of instructions which include the following: operational definitions of dimensions and categories, instructions regarding when observations are to be made, and instructions for making necessary tallies of observations. The number of dimensions and categories should not be excessive.

In an observational instrument, each dimension refers to a single behavior or attribute that is to be observed, such as playing, crying, laughing, and so on. Each dimension should be sufficiently operationally defined so that observers can agree that the behavior is or is not taking place. In addition, a dimension can be recorded in terms of the number of times it occurs, its intensity, or some quality of it. Thus, for example, playing can be classified in terms of the number of times it occurs in a specified time period, how actively it is engaged in, and whether it is solitary or involves others. Just as in the construction of forced-choice questions for questionnaires, observational categories should be mutually exclusive and exhaustive. Hence, whatever the classification scheme, categories should not overlap and, in addition, they should exhaust the range of possibilities along that dimension.

The actual recording of observations can be done on a check list, a tally sheet, or a rating scale. On a *check list*, behavioral dimensions are identified and observers indicate whether or not the behavior is observed. For example, ward attendants in a mental hospital may be asked to indicate whether given patients appear depressed, anxious, manic, and so on. Naturally, to use such a check list properly, attendants must be trained to accurately and reliably observe patients in terms of the foregoing categories.

A *tally sheet* requires that the observer mark each time a specific behavior occurs within a specified time period. Space is left for tallying up the total number of times the behavior is observed. An observer in a classroom, for example, may be asked to record the number of times in an hour that a student leaves his/her seat without permission, hits other children, and so on. Space will be left on the form for adding up the totals for each behavioral dimension observed.

Rating scales attempt to record the intensity or degree to which a dimension is exhibited. For example, an observer in a halfway house for former mental hospital patients may be asked to rate residents daily in terms of degrees of depression. The rating scale may be numerical, rating the presence of depression from 0 to 10, with 0 indicating no depression and 10, extreme depression. Or, specific non-numerical categories which are mutually exclusive and exhaustive may be provided, such as "not depressed," "mildly depressed," "moderately depressed," and "severely depressed." Here again, reliable use of such a rating scale requires that observers be instructed to apply these labels properly.

Since the construction of rating scales deserves a chapter in itself, we will provide one later in the book. Here, we will limit our remaining discussion of observational instruments to those which make use of checklists or tally sheets.

4. *Determining the Frequency of Observations*

For reasons of economy, in most clinical situations, observations must be made on a selective basis. For example, it might be clinically useful, but prohibitively expensive, to observe a disturbed child all day, every day, for a month. As a result, it is necessary to select a time sample. A *time sample* involves making observations at previously designated periods of time to obtain what is hopefully a representation of typical behavior. The times for observation may be selected randomly (see chapter 9), selected systematically (say every twenty minutes), or based on some strategic sense of the times that are most critical to the expression of problematic behaviors or emotional states.

As much as possible, the number of dimensions observed should be small enough and the number of observations made should be large enough to insure the reliability and validity of the observations made. However, if observers are not full-time observers, but must perform other roles, the number of observations should not interfere with their management of their other roles. If the demands of these other roles are not taken into account, the result will be fatigue, resentment and errors in judgment and in recording.

Overall, the observations should be broadly enough spaced so that recording them should not be overly laborious; yet they should be spaced narrowly enough to provide a fairly reliable representation of the situation to be observed. In a family situation, for example, recording parent-child conflicts on a weekly basis would lead to highly unreliable recording. Alternatively, monitoring conflicts every five minutes would be exhausting and unnecessarily precise. As with many other research issues, some balance must be struck between precision and practicality in constructing the instrument.

5. Choosing the Observer(s)

As we indicated earlier, any number of individuals may be involved in the collection of observational data. What is important, however, is that the observer have familiarity with the situation s/he is observing and with the dimensions and categories which are to be recorded. Consequently, only a trained clinician should be used to make complex clinical judgments. Alternatively, if the categories of behavior to be recorded are simple and part of everyone's day to day language and experience, nonexperts may be used. Accordingly, only trained clinicians should make judgments about whether a patient appears "manic." It does not take a professional, however, to record when someone is laughing.

Whatever his/her usual role in the situation to be observed, the observer should try to refrain from projecting his/her own biases and values on the behaviors observed. This is often very difficult. It is facilitated, however, by an instrument which contains clear instructions for making and recording observations, and which contains simple, behaviorally specific dimensions and categories. A final facilitator of valid and reliable observational data is training.

Even experienced clinicians may require training in order to do systematic observation.

6. *Training the Observers*

To properly use an observational instrument observers must be adequately trained. The amount of training necessary depends upon the complexity of the instrument and the clarity and specificity of dimensions, categories and instructions. The more complex or abstract the dimensions, the more training is required.

In training observers, they should first be instructed about the purpose of the instrument, how it is to be used, and the definitions of dimensions and categories. This can be accomplished through written instruction, oral presentations, and discussion for clarifying ambiguities or misunderstandings. Role-plays also can be helpful for simulating the situations to be observed and trying out the instrument.

Under no circumstances, however, should the observers be instructed about any hypotheses or hunches which are to be tested out with the instrument. This information is likely to bias their observations such that they will support their expectations. When there are no other observers to be used, and the individual who has developed the instrument is the one to implement it, a high level of self-control and objectivity is required so that the instrument is not used in a biased fashion to support a predetermined conclusion.

Among researchers, the ability to *refute* a hypothesis is highly valued. It is promoted by developing measures of each dimension that are clearly independent of each other so that predicted relationships between dimensions are honestly tested. Likewise, clinicians using observational instruments should strive to make objective observations so that it is possible, in fact, to demonstrate that their hunches are incorrect. If the instrument does not allow refutation, there is no legitimate reason to employ it. If it does make refutation possible, informational support for a prediction is that much more compelling.

The purpose of training observers is to standardize the use of the observational instrument, to reduce the number of errors and ambiguous recording of observations, to increase reliability, and to promote objectivity.

7. Pretesting the Observational Instrument

Before actually implementing an observational instrument, it should be pretested so that reliability estimates can be made and ambiguities in procedures can be ironed out. This can be accomplished by using the instrument on a trial basis in actual clinical situations, or with videotapes, audiotapes or role-plays of them. In pretesting, one should establish whether instructions are clear, whether the observers can use the instrument reliably and accurately, and whether use of the instrument causes undue fatigue or boredom. The latter elements, if present, will reduce reliability over time.

Having two independent observers to pretest the instrument is a useful procedure to help ensure reliability. However, that may not be practical in many clinical situations. If only one observer is used and s/he is observing many events over time, it is desirable to have another observer do spot checks of small segments of events occasionally to test reliability. If that is not practical, and events are recorded electronically, the observer can spot check his/her own reliability by recording an event and comparing the two data sets.

If events are not recorded electronically, they should be coded while the event is taking place. Coding done after the event is likely to be inaccurate and distorted. Some mechanical devices exist which make possible simultaneous coding and tallying of a small number of dimensions while the event is taking place. If none of the foregoing options are feasible, coding should be done *immediately* after the event has transpired.

8. Assessing the Validity of the Observational Instrument

In the context of systematic observation, *validity refers to the extent to which the observational instrument measures what it claims to measure. The two types of validity that are particularly relevant to observational in-*

struments are content and concurrent validity. Here, content validity refers to the *logical* connection between the observational instrument and the information pertinent to diagnostic assessment. This relationship can be established by having two or more experts review the dimensions and categories of these dimensions in the instrument to determine whether they constitute appropriate indicators of the clinically relevant information sought. Moreover, they should assess the extent to which this information is compatible with the theoretical orientation which prevails at the agency.

In this instance, *concurrent validity* refers to the extent to which the information generated by the observational instrument is consistent with information generated by other means. Thus, one would expect observational data regarding an applicant's level of anxiety to correspond with the applicant's self reports or with the reports of significant others in the applicant's environment. Although concurrent validity is difficult to demonstrate and may not be practically obtainable in many instances, we recommend, as a minimum, that an observational instrument should exhibit a high level of content validity before using it to make diagnostic assessments. See Rosen and Polansky (1975) for a more detailed discussion of validity of observation instruments.

9. Determining the Reliability of the Observational Instrument

To insure a high degree of reliability in the observations, observers should be trained in making and recording their observations in a nonbiased, unintrusive manner. When a number of observers are used, training and practice are necessary until a high level of inter-observer reliability is achieved. Here, *inter-observer* reliability refers to the extent to which two or more independent observers, observing the same situation without mutual consultation, using the same form, agree in their judgments and coding of the event. A simple index of inter-observer reliability is a percentage based on the number of agreements between the judges relative to the total number of judgments that they make, multiplied by 100. An index of 70–80 percent is generally regarded as fairly high.

Thus, two judges who agree in 8 out of 10 judgements exhibit an 80 percent index of inter-observer reliability.

It should be noted, however, that the larger the number of categories employed, the more difficult it is to reach such a high level of agreement. In other words, the greater the number of choices available for coding observations, the greater the probability of disagreement. Thus, if there are two categories for recording a dimension, by chance alone, observers are likely to agree 50 percent of the time. If there are three categories, chance observations would lead to agreement 33 percent of the time even if they were both blindfolded during observation sessions. Under such conditions, if there were four categories, they would probably agree 25 percent of the time, and so on.

In order to take the foregoing into account, one can proceed to test inter-observer reliability in two ways. The first involves collapsing contiguous categories of observation so that there are only two. Thus, if a rating scale includes four categories of anxiety (no anxiety, low anxiety, moderate anxiety, and high anxiety), and observations are roughly equally distributed among the categories, the no and low anxiety categories can be added together and treated as one category and the moderate and high anxiety categories added together and treated as another single category. Agreement will then be calculated on the basis of the two newly constructed categories. If the observations are not equally distributed among the categories, the split between the two should be done in such a way that roughly 50 percent of the observations fall into each of the newly constructed categories. Thus, if almost all the observations fall into the moderate and high anxiety categories, the no, low, and moderate anxiety categories should be collapsed and added together, and the high anxiety category should be kept intact.

Another procedure for roughly estimating reliability is used when there are more than two categories within a dimension and when the distribution of cases within categories is relatively equal. This procedure is based on the difference between the results that one would expect based on chance alone and an arbitrary standard set at 20 to 30 percent higher. Thus, for example, if a dimension has three categories one would expect agreement by chance alone in 33 percent of the observations. By adding an additional 20 to 30 percent, we can employ a *rough* criterion of 53 to 63 percent agreement as an acceptable standard of inter-observer reliability. Likewise, if there were four categories, we would expect agreement in 45 to 55 percent of the observations as an acceptable standard of interjudge reliability.

An important principle for estimating inter-observer reliability is that the observations are made independently, without the mutual collaboration of the observers. Under these conditions, high agreement among the observers indicates that they understand the dimensions and categories of observation, that the instructions for recording observations are clear, and that the format for recording the observations works. An observational system which is unreliable should not be used. Component parts of a system which are unreliable should not be used. Under these circumstances, unreliable systems or elements should be discarded, or the reasons for their unreliability should be identified and modified until acceptable levels of reliability are attained.

For each observer used, a high degree of intra-observer reliability is also desirable. In this context, *intra-observer reliability* refers to the extent to which a single observer repeatedly records the same event in the same way. With videotaped or other electronically recorded events, this is computed relatively easily by re-running the taped events, observing and coding them, and computing a percentage based on the number of agreements in judgements the individual observer makes, relative to the total number of judgments s/he makes, multiplied by 100. Here again a 70–80 percent reliability is generally required. For dimensions in which more than two categories exist, the techniques suggested earlier for estimating inter-observer reliability can be employed. In any case, there should be a sufficient time-lag between observational sessions, or a sufficient number of events to observe, so that the observer does not reproduce his/her observations from memory.

Finally, one should not assume that once established a high degree of reliability is easily maintained. Observers get tired or bored and their reliability declines. As they become more familiar with the situation to be observed, they become less attentive to new aspects and/or prejudge the course of events. To protect against these possibilities, spot checks should be done throughout the study. If observer boredom or fatigue is a problem, new observers should be employed. If a high degree of reliability is maintained throughout the study, one can have more confidence in the inferences drawn from the study's findings.

10. *Making the Observations*

In attempting to be as objective as possible, the observer should avoid influencing those he is observing. As much as possible, the observer's stance should be neutral and s/he should refrain from intervening in behalf of any of the participants in the situation observed. Even if s/he says nothing, however, his/her mere presence may significantly affect the behaviors of those observed. Because of this, it is advisable to give those who are to be observed some time to get used to the presence of the observer. Real data should not be collected until the observer is relatively confident that the participants in the situation are able to ignore his/her presence and recording activities.

HYPOTHETICAL ILLUSTRATION

Two school social workers, working in elementary school settings, frequently receive referrals from teachers of children who are described as "troublemakers," "immature," "disruptive," and the like. Over time, experience reveals that the teachers have a difficult time being specific about the behaviors to which these labels refer, and the frequency of these behaviors. At times, the social workers suspect that some children are being scapegoated by some teachers for reasons other than those reported and that these children's behaviors are not that different from the behaviors of their classmates.

The social workers decide to devise an observational instrument which will make it possible to record the frequency of behaviors which teachers find disruptive or indicative of "pathology" among those children referred. Such an instrument would make assessment of individual children possible as well as comparison of these children with some of their classmates. In addition, the instrument might indicate whether some teachers are less tolerant than others of normal youthful exuberance and/or are biased in other ways with regard to some children.

1. Determining What Is To Be Observed

The social workers want to observe the classroom behaviors of children who have been referred to them for treatment. In addition they want to be able to compare these children's behaviors with the behaviors of some of their classmates. For a starter, they are most concerned about monitoring the deportmental behaviors that teachers are most likely to describe as the bases for their referrals. These behaviors generally include speaking without permission, getting out of seat without permission, fighting with other children and refusal to comply with teacher's instructions.

2. Assessing the Availability of Existing Observational Instruments

In the library of a nearby social work school, the social workers discover a number of books and articles in the psychology and education field pertaining to "classroom management." Many of these publications contain highly complex observational instruments. The language in these publications is an additional problem to the social workers because it contains many technical behavioral modification terms and reflects a knowledge system with which the social workers are unfamiliar. Nevertheless, some components of some instruments are suggestive of observational dimensions which seem relevant. The social workers decide to use these elements as a guide to developing their own observational instrument.

3. Constructing the Observational Instrument

After talking with teachers and reviewing available literature, the social workers decide that there are four behavioral dimensions which they would like to include in their instrument: inappropriate talking, appropriate talking, being out of one's seat inappropriately, being out of one's seat appropriately. An "other" dimension is included to cover behaviors not included in the foregoing dimension. The social workers then begin to develop categories of behavior which fall into each of the dimensions. For example, inappropriate talking may include: answering a question without being recognized by the teacher, talking to a classmate when it is not permitted, and so on. Appropriate talking may include: answering a question when called upon by the teacher, talking to a classmate during a free period, etc. Being out of one's seat inappropriately may include: running around the class when one is supposed to be in one's seat, and going to the bathroom without permission. Appropriate leaving of one's seat may include: running an errand for the teacher, going to the bathroom with teacher's permission, and so on. Finally, "other" may include: quietly working in one's seat, reading, etc.

Once these dimensions and categories are specified and agreed upon, the social workers develop an observational form on which they can code, at regular intervals, the behaviors of children referred to them, as well as the behaviors of the neighboring children. The form might be very simple in which only the five dimensions would be coded for each child. Later, a more refined version might be developed in which the categories within these dimensions could be coded as well. In its present state, however, the specific categories only serve as instructions or indicators for coding each of the dimensions. The simplified form would look something like this:

Date: _____	Time: _____	
Referred child:	*Number of Times*	*Total*
Appropriate Talking:	/	1
Inappropriate Talking:	///	3
Appropriately Out of Seat:	/	1
Inappropriately Out of Seat:		
Other:	/	1

Neighboring Child A:		
Appropriate Talking:	*II*	2
Inappropriate Talking:		
Appropriately Out of Seat:	*I*	1
Inappropriately Out of Seat:	*I*	1
Other:	*I*	1
Neighboring Child B:		
Appropriate Talking:	*I*	1
Inappropriate Talking:	*III*	3
Appropriately Out of Seat:		
Inappropriately Out of Seat:		
Other:	*II*	2

With this form, individual observations are recorded by "hash marks" which are totalled for each category, for each child at the end of a day's observation.

4. Determining the Frequency of Observations

Based on other aspects of their workloads, the social workers determine that for pretesting purposes it would be possible for them to engage in three thirty-minute observational periods, on three successive days. On one day, observation will take place relatively early in the morning at 9:30 A.M. The next day, observation will begin at 11:30 A.M. On the final day, observation will be conducted in the afternoon at 2:00 P.M.

At the beginning of each observational period, the behavior of the referred child, the child immediately in front of him/her and the child immediately behind him/her will be recorded on the form. Using a stop watch, observers will repeat this process, every five minutes, resulting in six observations for each child during a thirty-minute observational period. At the end of each observational period, the results are tallied for each child. At the end of the three day period, these can be added together.

5. Choosing the Observers

During the pretesting stage of the instrument, both social workers are observing the same children in the same classroom, at the exact same times. This common observation of the same events is necessary for checking inter-observer reliability. In other situations, it might be appropriate to have the teacher, a student teacher, or a teacher's aide conducting simultaneous observations. Once any of these individuals becomes well-trained in the use of the instrument s/he may be used to collect the primary information without the presence of a dual observer.

6 and 7. Training Observers and Pretesting the Observational Instrument

Since the social workers were themselves the authors of the observational forms and the observers, no additional training was necessary. However, after pretesting the form, they discussed the few instances of disagreement. This led to a more refined definition of what constitutes appropriate and inappropriate talking behavior. These were the dimensions along which they disagreed most.

Should the workers decide to have others use this instrument, they will need to offer training sessions and to conduct reliability tests of the new observers' use of the instrument. However, if this is not their intention, the instrument is ready to be used by each of them for diagnostic assessment of the children referred to them.

8. Assessing the Validity of the Observational Instrument

The social workers judge the instrument to be valid based on the logical connection between the instrument and the behaviors that are of concern to the teachers and social workers. However, to the extent that there are vast discrepancies between teacher reports concerning specific children's behaviors and the information generated by the forms, the question of concurrent validity arises. Thus, one possible explanation is that the form has low concurrent validity and needs to be refined further. The other possibility is that the teacher's reports are not valid and are, in fact, based on a biased perception of the particular child's behavior. To deal with this problem, the social worker may want to do another round of observations first, before refining the instrument further. If the results based on the structured observations remain consistently at variance with the teacher's reports, then the teacher should be presented with this information and the social worker's interventions may be directed towards the teacher.

9. Determining the Reliability of the Observational Instrument

After the pretest of the observational instrument, the social workers compare their results on each of the dimensions for each of the youngsters observed, for each observation session. By dividing the number of agreements by the total number of observations for each dimension and multiplying by 100, they establish an 80 percent or higher inter-observer reliability for each dimension. Consequently, they assume that they can each employ the instrument reliably enough to use it independently for diagnostic-assessment purposes.

10. Making the Observations

In order to avoid influencing the situation as much as possible, the social workers first asked permission of the teachers in whose rooms they would conduct their observations. In addition, they would spend about twenty minutes in the classroom the day before and the day after they conducted their systematic observation. During these before and after days, however, they would also carefully observe the behaviors of the children they were to be systematically observing in order to get a sense of whether their behaviors were generally comparable on the days that systematic observations were conducted. Finally, before each set of structured observations were conducted, the social workers would spend ten minutes in the classroom so that teachers and students would be used to their presence and presumably behave in their natural manner when the systematic observations would begin.

EXERCISE

With a colleague, observe a videotape of a clinical interview. After the tape is finished, each of you write a narrative statement describing the level of anxiety which the client exhibits. Indicate the bases upon which you came to the conclusion you did. Next, devise a systematic observational instrument for recording the number of times the client makes statements or gestures which indicate anxiety. Replay and code the tape. Wait a day and repeat the playing and coding activity. Compute the inter-observer and intra-observer reliability of the instrument. How reliable is it? Which form of reliability is higher?

SELECTED BIBLIOGRAPHY

Bales, Robert F., "A Set of Categories for the Analysis of Small Group Interaction," in Dennis P. Forcese and Stephen Richer, eds., *Stages of Social Research* (Englewood Cliffs, N.J.: Prentice-Hall, 1970), pp. 216–23.

Becker, Howard S. and Blanche Geer, "Participant Observation and Interviewing: A Comparison," in William J. Filstead, ed., *Qualitative Methodology* (Chicago: Markham, 1970), pp. 133–42.

Cataldo, Michael F., and Todd R. Risley, "Evaluation of Living Environments: The Manifest Description of Ward Activities," in Park O. Davidson, Frank W. Clark, Leo A. Hamerlynck, eds., *Evaluation of Behavioral Programs* (Champaign, Ill.: Research Press, 1974), pp. 201–222.

Epstein, Irwin and Tony Tripodi, *Research Techniques for Program Planning, Monitoring, and Evaluation* (New York: Columbia University Press, 1977), pp. 42–54 and 70–76.

Goldstein, Harris K., *Research Standards and Methods for Social Workers* (New Orleans: Hauser Press, 1963), pp. 45–60.

Howe, Michael W., "Using Clients' Observations in Research," in *Social Work* (January 1976), 21(1):28–33.

Liberman, Robert P., William J. DeRisi, Larry W. King, Thad A.

Eckman, and David Wood, "Behavioral Measurement in a Community Mental Health Center," in Park O. Davidson, Frank W. Clark, Leo A. Hamerlynck, eds., *Evaluation of Behaviorial Programs* (Champaign, Ill.: Research Press, 1974), pp. 103–40.

Riley, Matilda W., *Sociological Research II, Exercises and Manual* (New York: Harcourt, Brace and World, 1963), pp. 2–4 and 14.

Rosen, Sidney and Norman A. Polansky, "Observation of Social Interaction," in Norman A. Polansky, ed., *Social Work Research* (rev. ed.; Chicago: University of Chicago Press, 1975), pp. 154–81.

5

THE SELECTION OF TREATMENT TECHNIQUES

Once a diagnostic assessment has been made, the clinical social worker is faced with the task of selecting a treatment or intervention strategy. Some social workers rely completely on their previous training or practice experience as a basis for their selection. Others may base their decisions on the treatment traditions of the agency in which they are employed. An alternative source of intervention ideas is the research literature. Here, hypotheses about the effectiveness of specific intervention techniques and the conditions under which they work best are given more rigorous testing than they receive in many practice settings.

Practice-relevant research offers knowledge at four distinct levels: (1) hypotheses predicting relationships between practice techniques and client outcomes; (2) descriptive knowledge about intervention techniques, client characteristics, and agency settings; (3) correlational knowledge concerning the statistical relationships between intervention and outcome; and (4) cause-effect knowledge which documents a causal relationship between intervention and outcome. The first level of knowledge is highly speculative. However, as one moves from level (2) to level (4), the knowledge becomes less speculative and more certain. Thus, it is easier to hypothesize about the relationship between intervention and outcome than to demonstrate that the former has a clear and specific impact on the latter. Nevertheless, knowledge taken from all four of these levels can be extremely useful in selecting practice interventions.

This chapter provides principles for critically reviewing research from each of the foregoing levels. It focuses on the use of available research literature for the location, assessment, and selection of intervention strategies.

ASSESSING TREATMENT TECHNIQUES

Before discussing research assessment principles, it is important to remind the reader that clinical practice rarely conforms with the neat, rational, time-ordered, "heuristic" model of diagnosis, treatment, and evaluation which we are employing. Hence, diagnostic assessments, rather than taking place prior to and independent of treatment decisions, are themselves likely to be affected by the treatment techniques with which clinicians feel most comfortable. In emergencies, for example, treatment may necessarily begin before a diagnostic assessment has been completed. And, most clinicians simply do not have the time to review the research literature each time they have to make a treatment decision.

Despite these understandable departures from the ideal model, principles of research review and assessment are not frivolous luxury items for the responsible clinician. They can be applied in a range of contexts in which questions about treatment are raised. Even if they are not used on a case-by-case basis, assessment principles can be employed in reviewing research concerning practice interventions directed toward problems which affect whole classes of agency clients, for example, alcoholics, drug addicts, depressives, and the like. Here, systematic review of the literature testing various treatment approaches can lead to the selection of intervention strategies for all clients experiencing a particular problem.

Principles of research assessment can be used as well for evaluating treatment techniques which are described in places other than the research literature. Thus, the same principles can be used to assess oral reports, workshops, written agency reports, and other less formal efforts to describe treatment interventions and their effects.

Finally, research assessment principles can be used to select treatment monitoring and evaluation instruments. These devices themselves need to be described, assessed, and evaluated before they are implemented in clinical settings.

PRINCIPLES FOR ASSESSING TREATMENT TECHNIQUES

1. Specifying the Problem

The clinical social worker should turn to the research literature when there is a felt need for knowledge about existing or new techniques related to a client's or a client group's problems. This felt need may come about as a result of the clinician's confrontation with a new problem, one with which s/he has never worked. Or, there may be a sense of dissatisfaction with the level of effectiveness of previous efforts to treat the problem. This dissatisfaction may arise in an individual case, in which a particular client is not responding positively to treatment. Alternatively, it may be the result of persistent problems in effectively treating a whole class of client problems.

Whatever the source of the need for new knowledge, the search should begin with a specification of the problem, its pervasiveness, its frequency of occurrence, as well as the conditions under which it is likely to occur or not occur. In addition, there should be a complete description of the characteristics of the clientele involved, the treatment techniques which have been tried in the past, and any evidence of success which may have been achieved. The foregoing information will make it possible to locate relevant literature and to assess whether alternative treatment strategies which are described in the literature are any better than what has already been tried by the practitioner.

2. Locating Relevant Research Literature

Having specified the problem, one should then locate literature bearing on social work or related clinical efforts to treat the problem. One way to locate relevant studies is to use the journals or abstracts described earlier in our chapter on locating diagnostic assessment instruments. Current social-work-related studies may also be located by perusal of the annual title indexes of practice journals such as the *American Journal of Orthopsychiatry*, the *Journal of Applied Behavior Analysis*, the *Journal of Clinical Social Work*, and the *Journal of Consulting Psychology, Psychiatry, Social Casework, Social Work, Social Service Review*, and the like.

In addition to journals, abstracts, and books that are located in libraries, current research on practice techniques may be presented at workshops devoted to particular practice problems, in papers given at professional conferences, as well as in open lectures given at universities and other institutions.

3. Getting an Overview of the Research

Before reading a research study in depth, one should first skim it to get an overview of the material presented to determine whether the study deals with relevant intervention strategies and problem formulations. This is facilitated by reading the abstract which may appear at the beginning of articles published in many journals.

If the material is to be presented orally, in a workshop or a lecture, one can frequently get a sense of the presentation's relevance from advertisements, program guides and references to the presenter's recent publications which may be included in advance advertising.

4. Specifying the Intervention Techniques

If the material appears to be relevant, one should then specify the treatment techniques which are discussed. If they are vague, ambiguous and unspecifiable, they are not likely to be successfully adopted. Any success reported is likely to be a consequence of charismatic qualities of the persons employing the intervention. If, on the other hand, the techniques are clearly described, the clinician must consider whether they are compatible with the practice context in which s/he is employed, the theoretical orientation and professional values which s/he brings to the setting, the particular characteristics of the client or clientele which is served, and so on.

Having determined that the approach described is ethically acceptable and technically applicable, one should answer the following questions: how often is the technique employed; who uses it; what are the specifics of the treatment technique; under what conditions is it employed; is it used with individuals, families and/or groups; what obligations or expectations does it put upon clients and social workers; what are the training requirements for social workers employing the technique; what are the characteristics of the clients on whom the techniques are employed?

Answering these questions may require further research into previous publications by the author or speaker. These questions may be asked directly, if the materials are presented orally as in a workshop. It is essential, however, that the clinician establish that the interventions described deal with problems similar to those with which the clinician is trying to cope, that they are employable in the clinician's own agency setting, and that they are compatible with his/her professional values.

5. Criteria of Effectiveness and Efficiency

Once the intervention strategies have been clearly identified, one should then determine the criteria used in assessing the effectiveness of the techniques employed. This is not solely a technical research issue. The effectiveness of treatment can be viewed from the perspectives of different consumers. What is viewed as effective by one consumer may be trivial to another (Hiebert 1974).

In clinical practice, effectiveness must be judged in terms of the client's perspective, the clinician's perspective, the perspectives of significant others in the client's environment, and from the perspective of society. Needless to say, these occasionally conflict with each other.

From the client's perspective, effectiveness can involve positively valued changes in mood, self-experiences or behaviors of the client, or experiences or behaviors of significant others. A client may seek change in his/her environment. Alternatively, s/he may seek to feel more comfortable with an unchangeable set of circumstances.

From the standpoint of significant others, success may mean very different things. To family members, for example, treatment may be judged effective to the extent that a client is less of an emotional or economic burden. A client who has desired to become more assertive as a function of individual therapy, may be perceived by family members as less pleasant, less compliant, and so on. A homosexual client who has become more comfortable with a condition which s/he does not wish to change, may be perceived as an embarrassment to family members once this has been openly acknowledged.

The social worker's theoretical orientation, as well, may emphasize different notions of effectiveness. Analytically oriented social workers particularly value verbalized insight. Behavior therapists emphasize changes in behaviors. Social workers engaged in advocacy attempt to change environmental conditions, and so on.

Finally, from the standpoint of society, success may be more a question of cost, or the efficiency of treatment intervention and whether the client presents a threat to him/herself, others, or to property belonging to others.

Recognizing that these conflicts exist, the clinical social worker must regard the client's perspective first and judge treatment techniques first and foremost by whether they produce results that are satisfying to the client. Ideally, of course, the social worker should seek treatment techniques which are mutually satisfying to significant others, to the clinician him/herself, and to the larger society as well.

In addition, the social worker should consider the extent to which information is provided about the effectiveness of the technique as compared with other techniques. Moreover, to what extent does it provide information about the cost of achieving a given level of effectiveness? A technique may be highly effective but prohibitive in cost. Finally, one should ask how the efficiency of the technique, that is, the relationship between effectiveness and cost, compares with the efficiency of other intervention strategies.

6. Assessing the Level of Knowledge Produced

Research on practice has as its objective the production of quantitative knowledge that is descriptive, hypothetical, correlational or causal. Qualitative hypothetical knowledge is important for generating new approaches to practice but falls outside the focus of this chapter. Such knowledge is generated by hunch, intuition, or guesswork. It may be highly inventive and original, but unless it is subjected to evaluation we do not recommend its adoption.

Ascertaining the level of quantitative knowledge produced will affect the criteria for evidence which should be used in assessing effectiveness. To assess quantitative hypotheses one must consider their internal logic and the extent to which they are consistent with previous theory and research. To assess descriptive, correlational and causal studies, one must consider the extent to which measurement accuracy, reliability and validity have been achieved. To assess correlational studies, one must consider not only measurement accuracy, reliability and validity, but the evidence of statistical association as well. Finally, in assessing cause-effect studies, one must consider measurement accuracy, reliability and validity, statistical association and, in addition, evidence of internal control. Each of these criteria of assessment is discussed in subsequent sections of this chapter.

7. Assessing Measurement Accuracy, Reliability, and Validity

Whatever the level of knowledge sought, the quality of a research study or report depends to a large degree on the accuracy, reliability, and validity of the measures it employs. In assessing the effectiveness of treatment techniques, these criteria are applied to the measures of effectiveness which are employed.

In this context, measurement accuracy refers to the degree of freedom from error in the process of measuring treatment effectiveness. It concerns itself with whether or not mistakes have been made in the clerical processing or tabulation of the data. Although these errors may not be directly observable, one can get a sense of the efforts made by the researcher to guard against such error.

Accuracy also pertains to the achievement of measurement scales with mutually exclusive and exhaustive categories of effectiveness. In research on the effectiveness of treatment techniques, three kinds of scales are generally used: nominal, ordinal, and interval. *Nominal scales* are the simplest. In these simple scales, data are classified into two or more mutually exclusive and exhaustive categories that imply no rank ordering or hierarchy. Thus, the information that after a given type of intervention some cases are still in treatment, and some are terminated, is a nominal scale in which the categories do not necessarily imply which is the preferred outcome. It does, however, describe an important piece of information.

Ordinal scales present two or more mutually exclusive and exhaustive categories in an order or hierarchy of some kind. A scale describing clients as not improved or improved would be the simplest kind of ordinal scale. A slightly more refined ordinal scale might describe clients as not improved, somewhat improved, and greatly improved.

Interval scales are similar to ordinal scales except that they are even more refined. They are calibrated so that the units of measurement along the scale are equidistant from each other. These categories are also mutually exclusive and exhaustive. A scale describing the frequency of specific problematic behaviors such as drug use, incidents of child abuse, and the like, may be expressed in the form of an interval scale. On this scale the distance between one and two incidents is viewed as significant as the difference between five and six incidents. A reduction of one unit on any point of the scale would be viewed as equally effective.

The type of scale employed in measuring both intervention and effectiveness will determine which statistical methods are most appropriate in correlating treatment techniques with outcomes. Interventions as well as outcomes can be expressed in norminal, ordinal, or interval scales. There are rules about the kinds of statistical measures which can be used in assessing their effects. For example, a phi correlation can be calculated if the intervention and/or the outcome is expressed in a nominal scale. When both intervention and outcome are ordinal scales, a rank-order correlation (rho) is most appropriate. Pearson's r correlation is most appropriate when both intervention and outcome are interval scales. A full discussion of these statistical measures and their uses is outside the scope of this book, but can be found within any standard introductory text on statistical methods.

Reliability, as we indicated in earlier chapters, can be assessed in a number of different ways (intra-observer, inter-observer, split-half, test-retest) and can be expressed in the form of percentage agreement or correlation coefficients. Just as in other contexts, one would expect reliability measures indicating 70 percent or higher agreement or .70 or higher correlations when comparisons are made between scales with two categories. Lower reliability scores might be expected if the number of categories were higher. Higher scores might be expected in split-half tests. In assessing the evidence of the effectiveness of treatment over time, however, it is essential that test-retest reliability be established. In this way we can be assured that indications of client improvement are the result of treatment rather than of the nonreliability of the measurement instrument itself.

The validity of the measurement instrument is equally important in assessing treatment effectiveness. Here, what is most important is that the measures of outcome used are as closely related to the treatment objectives as possible. Beyond the issue of content validity just raised, is predictive validity. Ideally, measures which show good predictive validity could be used to make inferences about the extent to which successful treatment outcomes persist over time.

Taking the issues of accuracy, reliability and validity together, it should be emphasized that studies which do not indicate sufficient attention to these issues should be treated as generating hypothetical knowledge rather than as being descriptive, correlational or causal. In other words, unless measurement accuracy, reliability, and validity are reasonably demonstrated, the knowledge produced should be considered as hypotheses worthy of future testing rather than as fact.

8. Assessing the Empirical Relationship Between Intervention and Outcome

Only in correlational and cause-effect studies is it possible to test the strength of the relationship between treatment and client outcome. In assessing the knowledge generated in these studies, however, it is important to consider the strength, direction, and predictability of the relationship between the intervention strategy and the results obtained.

The *strength of the relationship* is determined by the degree of association between the treatment and the desired outcome. It may be expressed in percentage differences, mean differences, or correlation coefficients. A study that employs percentage differences would indicate the strength of the relationship through one or more of the following comparisons: the percentage difference in desired outcome between those who received the intervention and a matched group that received no intervention (that is, a control group); the percentage difference in a desired outcome between groups that received different interventions (that is, contrast groups); the percentage difference in a desired outcome within a group before and after receiving the intervention (that is, a group serving as its own control); and the percentage difference in a desired outcome between a group that received an authentic intervention and a group that received a placebo intervention.

On outcome measures that are expressed in numerical scores—for example, an anxiety scale, a reading score, and the like—comparisons may be made by showing the differences in the arithmetic averages or mean scores between the group that received the intervention and any of the comparison groups mentioned above.

The strength of the relationship between intervention and outcome may also be expressed in the form of a correlation coefficient. As we stated in chapter 3, most correlation coefficients can vary in strength from 0.0 to 1.0. However, in assessing the strength of a relationship between intervention and outcome, one would not ordinarily expect correlations as high as one would for a test of reliability. A correlation of .25 would be considered strong enough to justify the generalization that an intervention had some association with the desired outcome. A correlation of .50 would be considered substantial and a correlation of .70 would be considered very high.

Some correlation coefficients (for example, Pearson's *r*, Spearman's rho) are expressed in positive or negative terms. These measures range from −1.00 to +1.00 and indicate the *direction* as well as the strength of the relationship between intervention and outcome. A negative correlation would indicate an *inverse* relationship between the two. That would mean, the greater the amount of intervention, the lower the score on the measurement of client outcome. Alternatively, a positive correlation would indicate a *direct* relationship between intervention and the outcome measure. Thus, if treatment were designed to reduce feelings of depression, one would hope for a strong, inverse correlation between intervention and outcome. On the other hand, if an intervention was designed to increase assertiveness, one would hope for a strong direct correlation.

One advantage of correlation coefficients, as compared with percentage and mean difference data, is that with a correlation coefficient it is possible to approximate the predictability of a given outcome when one knows the correlation between intervention and outcome. *Predictability* refers to the percentage of the variation on the outcome that can be explained by the intervention. By squaring the correlation coefficient and multiplying by 100 one gets an approximation of predictability. So, for example, if a study concluded that there was a correlation of .50 between participation in a conjoint therapy program and marital satisfaction scores, by squaring the correlation coefficient and multiplying by 100 one would predict that approximately 25 percent of the change in marital satisfaction scores was accounted for by participation in the conjoint therapy program.

9. Assessing Empirical Generality

Empirical generality refers to whether the findings of a study can be generalized to other comparable practice situations and to other populations of clients and practitioners. The use of random sampling techniques (to be more fully discussed later in the book) increases the likelihood that findings can be generalized by making possible the computation of measures of statistical significance of the relationship between intervention and outcome. *Statistical significance* refers to whether the relationship between intervention and outcome found in the population sample studied reflects a true relationship in the population to which one would like to generalize and from which the sample population was drawn. This is important because the apparent success of an intervention may be the result of chance fluctuations. Assuming the study population was randomly selected, on the basis of the laws of probability one can calculate statistical significance by means of various measures of association between intervention and outcome, for example, chi-square, for percentage-differences and t-tests for mean-differences. Social scientists have generally accepted findings that are significant at the .05 level or lower (.01, .001) as indicative of a statistically significant relationship. This means that the findings of the study were such that given the size of the population studied, they could have occurred only 5 times in 100 by chance alone. Naturally, findings at the .01 level would be even more certain. That would indicate that the empirical relationship demonstrated between intervention and outcome could have occured only 1 time in 100 by chance, and so on.

Measures of statistical significance can be misleading, however, because of the manner in which they are calculated. The larger the study population is, the weaker the relationship between intervention and outcome needs to be to be judged statistically significant.

For example, in a study with a sample of 100, a 35 percent change in an outcome measure may be required to attain statistical significance. In a similar study with a sample population of 1,000 a change of only 3 percent in the outcome measure may be required. In other words, with a large enough study population a weak correlation may still be statistically significant. Consequently, measures of statistical significance tell us more about whether we can generalize from the sample studied to the population it represents than they tell us about the strength of a relationship between intervention and outcome. Thus, the foregoing findings would tell us that in the study of 100 we can assume that if the intervention were applied to the population from which the sample was selected a moderate rate of success would be likely to occur. In the study of 1,000, statistical significance would suggest that if the intervention were applied to the larger population a low rate of success would be likely to occur. Therefore, statistical significance does not necessarily imply success.

Another way of assessing the level of empirical generality is to determine whether the findings of the study have been replicated elsewhere in other studies. If one is able to locate comparable studies and they yield findings of similar strength and direction, one can have greater confidence in the knowledge one has concerning the results of a given intervention. In studies of a single subject or case, Hersen and Barlow (1976) suggest that there should be at least 3 successful replications with similar clients, therapists, problem situations and therapeutic interventions before empirical generality is inferred. In correlational studies, there should be consistency with reference to the strength, direction and statistical significance of the correlations.

Finally, in making decisions about whether study findings can be applied to another population, one should consider the extent to which the characteristics of practitioners, clientele, setting and intervention match those in one's own agency or practice context. Random sampling in the study itself increases the likelihood that the study findings can be generalized to the population from which the sample was selected. Similarity between one's own practice context and that of the study increase the likelihood that the study findings can be generalized to one's own situation.

10. Assessing Internal Control

In order to establish that a cause-effect relationship actually exists between an intervention strategy and a desired outcome, one must rule out alternative possible explanations for the outcome. This is accomplished through *internal control* procedures.

There are several questions one should ask to assess the adequacy of internal controls in a study. First, are the changes observed directly traceable to the intervention? Second, is there evidence that the changes followed rather than preceded the intervention? Third, is there evidence that changes are not simply the result of growth or maturity or other external factors influencing the research subjects? Fourth, is it clear that observed positive changes are not a consequence of a desire for positive changes on the part of the researcher? In other words, are the measures of success fair and unbiased? Fifth, is there evidence that the observed changes are not a result of the subjects' desire to please the researcher, that is, what is generally referred to as the "Hawthorne effect"? And finally, is there evidence that observed changes are the result of an authentic intervention rather than a response to a falsely perceived intervention, that is, a "placebo effect"?

Many of these questions are dealt with in research studies through the use of control groups and the use of statistical procedures for testing alternative explanations. Moreover, by limiting the subject population to single categories of individuals—for example, adolescents, females, Puerto-Ricans, or middle-income clients—one can rule out the possible confounding effects of age, sex, ethnicity, or social class on a given outcome.

11. Applying Different Assessment Criteria to Different Levels of Knowledge

The foregoing assessment criteria should be applied differentially, depending upon the level of knowledge which a study is attempting to generate. The lower the level of knowledge produced, the less stringent will be the assessment criteria. Thus, descriptive studies require only a moderate degree of confidence in measurement accuracy, reliability and validity; whereas cause-effect studies require relatively high confidence in the criteria.

Second, the level of empirical generality will determine whether study findings should be treated as fact or simply as interesting hypotheses for future testing. When the empirical generality is low, the knowledge produced should be treated as hypothetical. Only when empirical generality is high, can one infer that a comparable cause-effect relationship exists between intervention and outcome for comparable populations and practice situations. When *both* empirical generality and relationship strength are high, then one can feel assured of the sufficient demonstration of cause-effect knowledge such that the intervention described can be successfully applied to one's own practice population. At the very least, clinical social workers should require correlational knowledge before applying a technique discussed in a research study. Interventions discussed in studies which generate descriptive or hypothetical knowledge should be applied with caution. Moreover, these applications should themselves be carefully evaluated. Strategies for evaluating practice interventions are discussed in the third section of the book.

12. Assessing Possibilities of Implementation

In considering the possible adoption of an intervention strategy discussed in the research literature, one should ask the following questions:

a. Is the intervention strategy discussed compatible with the theoretical orientation which prevails at the agency?

b. Is the intervention strategy more effective and less costly than strategies that are currently in use?

c. What staff, training, and equipment needs would be required if the new strategy were to be adopted?

d. How likely is it that agency superiors and staff colleagues would support this innovation?

The answers to these questions should be weighed in the light of the evidence presented in the research literature. In this way more rational decision-making concerning intervention approaches can be achieved.

HYPOTHETICAL ILLUSTRATION

In a problem pregnancy counseling program serving low-income women, staff have observed that some women who come for counseling are so anxious that counseling efforts are thwarted. Traditionally, these women have been given tranquilizing drugs by attending physicians to reduce their anxiety and to make them amenable to counseling. However, for those women who intend to carry through their pregnancies, there is concern about the impact of these drugs on the developing fetus. For these women as well as those having abortions, there is concern about the dulling and depressive impact of the tranquilizers and the extent to which the tranquilizers inhibit direct confrontation with the sources of their extreme anxiety.

1. Specifying the Problem

The problem is defined as whether there are any nonmedical interventions which can be successfully used to reduce extreme and debilitating anxiety in a population of pregnant women.

2. Locating Relevant Research Literature

Using the concepts of "anxiety" and "anxiety reduction" as key concepts, relevant literature is located in public health, medical and social work journals through the abstract journals and guides to periodical literature. Although this literature does not deal with anxiety reduction in pregnant women, there is a sizable literature describing anxiety reduction techniques in a variety of settings, with a variety of types of subjects. One technique, in particular, is researched in a number of studies, that is, deep muscle relaxation.

3. Getting an Overview of the Research

These research studies fully describe the intervention technique as well as the measures of anxiety which are employed. The articles are clearly written, provide empirical evidence, and include detailed references for follow-up on more technical points. A quick skim of 5 studies found indicates that 4 out of 5 conclude that there is a demonstrable association between deep muscle relaxation and anxiety reduction. These findings warrant a more intensive study of the articles.

4. Specifying the Intervention Technique

The technique of deep muscle relaxation is described in detail by Wolpe and Lazarus (1966). It requires six twenty-minute interviews and involves practice by the subject for two fifteen-minute periods per day. The subject is verbally instructed in how to relax different sets of muscles in a progressive manner, from interview to interview. The technique is fully and clearly described.

5. Criteria of Effectiveness and Efficiency

All of the studies employed a questionnaire about self-reported anxiety (the Taylor Manifest Anxiety Scale) to assess the success of intervention. In addition, some studies employed a physiological test of anxiety based on skin response. Changes in both of these types of scores before and after deep muscle relaxation training were regarded as criteria of effectiveness. No direct efforts at measuring efficiency were reported.

6. Assessing the Level of Knowledge Generated

All the studies reported correlational knowledge that was presumably generalizable. Hence the criteria of measurement accuracy, reliability, validity, strength of relationship, and empirical generality were relevant to apply. To the extent that information about internal control was reported, more powerful inferences about the findings might have been drawn.

7. Assessing Measurement Accuracy, Reliability, and Validity

Procedures for scoring subjects were monitored carefully and described in these studies. Some studies reported test-retest reliability for self-reported anxiety scores ranging from .70 to .90. Test-retest reliability of the skin response scores were reported between .60 and .80. Validity was assessed in two ways. First, content validity was established through an examination of the content of the questions in the self-reported anxiety scale. Next, concurrent validity was reported in some studies in which correlations between .50 and .60 were found between the self-reported anxiety scale and the skin response scores. Hence there was moderate to high measurement accuracy, reliability and validity.

8. Assessing the Empirical Relationship Between Intervention and Outcome

Each study compared a treatment group with a control group which did not receive treatment. Each group was measured before treatment and after the treatment group received muscle relaxation counseling. All treatment groups showed greater reduction in anxiety on all measures than did the control groups. Negative correlations averaging −.40 were reported between muscle relaxation counseling and anxiety. Hence, there was some empirical evidence to suggest that deep muscle relaxation treatment was inversely associated with anxiety.

9. Assessing Empirical Generality

Four out of five studies reported statistically significant findings and the fifth study, though not statistically significant, reported findings in the desired direction. Although no procedures for random sampling were reported, all studies dealt exclusively with female subjects, from middle-class backgrounds, and male therapists. Thus, there is some basis for generalizing to the program population based on the sex of the subject; however, the differences in class background between study subjects and program clientele, and the fact that program staff are all women suggest that the level of empirical generality to the program is low.

10. Assessing Internal Control

Although the studies employ control groups, no efforts are described to test alternative explanations for the reduction in anxiety after treatment.

11. Applying Assessment Criteria to Level of Knowledge

Since the studies report correlational knowledge, indicate low empirical generality and reveal no direct efforts to assess internal control, the findings generated must be treated as hypotheses to be tested in other practice contexts. Thus, if the technique is to be tried in the program, it should be carefully evaluated.

12. Assessing Possibility of Implementation

It is determined that the intervention technique described is relatively specific and can be learned quickly in a one-day workshop conducted by an expert in this field. The technique is theoretically and ethically acceptable to the agency and is not very costly in terms of training or implementation. As a result, the technique is adopted on a trial basis subject to systematic evaluation.

EXERCISE

Identify a practice problem which you feel your current intervention reportoire does not effectively treat. Search the research literature for studies which describe other intervention techniques for dealing with this problem. Assess these studies using the principles described in this chapter. Do they warrant adoption of the intervention strategy described? Under what conditions?

SELECTED BIBLIOGRAPHY

Campbell, Donald T. and Julian C. Stanley, *Experimental and Quasi-Experimental Designs for Research* (Chicago: Rand McNally, 1963), pp. 3–6.

Epstein, Irwin and Tony Tripodi, *Research Techniques for Program Planning, Monitoring, and Evaluation* (New York: Columbia University Press, 1977), pp. 29–41.

Goldstein, Harris K., *Research Standards and Methods for Social Workers* (New Orleans: Hauser, 1963), pp. 303–13.

Hardyck, Curtis and Lewis F. Petrinovich, *Understanding Research in the Social Sciences* (Philadelphia: W. B. Saunders, 1975).

Hersen, Michel and David H. Barlow, *Single Case Experimental Designs* (New York: Pergamon, 1976), pp. 317–74.

Hiebert, Siegfried, "Who Benefits from the Program? Criteria Selection," in Park O. Davidson, Frank W. Clark and Leo A. Hamerlynck, eds., *Evaluation of Behavioral Programs* (Champaign, Ill.: Research Press, 1974), pp. 33–54.

Huff, Darrell, *How to Lie With Statistics* (New York: Norton, New York, 1954), pp. 11–26.

Tripodi, Tony, *Uses and Abuses of Social Research in Social Work* (New York: Columbia University Press, 1974), pp. 43–106.

Tripodi, Tony, Phillip Fellin, and Henry J. Meyer, *The Assessment of Social Research* (Itasca, Ill.: F. E. Peacock, 1969), pp. 6–8 and 60–93.

Weber, Ruth E. and Norman A. Polansky, "Evaluation" in *Social Work Research* (rev. ed.; Chicago: University of Chicago Press, 1975), pp. 182–201.

Wechsler, Henry, Helen Z. Reinherz, and Donald D. Dobbin, *Social Work Research in the Human Services* (New York: Human Services Press, 1976), pp. 203–86.

Wolpe, Joseph, and Arnold A. Lazarus, *Behavior Therapy Techniques* (London: Pergamon, 1966), pp. 54–101.

Part Two

TREATMENT IMPLEMENTATION AND MONITORING

Treatment implementation is the second phase of clinical social work practice. Simply stated, treatment implementation involves carrying out an intervention plan with a client. Monitoring is the process by which judgments are made about the extent to which the client is actually receiving the prescribed intervention in a manner which is consistent with prior planning, agency and professional standards, and the contractual agreement between client and social worker.

Effective treatment monitoring involves setting treatment standards, gathering and analyzing data concerning the attainment of these standards, assessing any discrepancies between planned and actual performance on the part of the clinician and/or the client, and making decisions to continue, stop, or modify the implementation strategy depending on the foregoing assessment.

Assessment standards and sources of monitoring data may vary. Standards for intervention, for example, can originate in practice norms articulated by professional associations (NASW, ACSW), agency rules and procedures, or treatment contracts. Likewise, information about compliance with these standards may come from process recordings, a social worker's clinical observations, client self-reports, or the observations of significant others in the client's or the social worker's environment.

Through the process of treatment implementation and monitoring, judgments can be made about the quality, comprehensiveness, and continuity of treatment. These types of treatment assessments are particularly important in problem areas in which the ultimate impact of treatment is difficult to assess. They are valuable, as well, in assessing worker performance in treatment modes which have proven to be successful and do not require outcome evaluation.

Wherever possible, treatment monitoring should be based upon valid, reliable, and representative information feedback to the social worker and/or the social worker's supervisor. Research concepts and techniques can facilitate the systematic collection, analysis and interpretation of this information. In addition, data which are collected systematically from a number of comparable cases can be aggregated for the purpose of making generalizations about treatment with certain types of cases.

In this section, we describe the tasks and decisions associated with the treatment implementation stage. Next, we discuss ways in which research monitoring can inform this stage of practice. The three chapters in this section describe in detail the use of specific research concepts and techniques for treatment monitoring.

Before proceding however, we should remind the reader of two things. First, the research concepts and techniques detailed in this section are not solely applicable to treatment monitoring. Indeed, they are useful in diagnostic assessment and in the evaluation of treatment outcomes as well. Second, the reader is reminded that our phase model of clinical practice is only a heuristic device. Actual practice is not nearly as logically distinct or linear. Thus, for example, in practice initial diagnostic assessments and treatment formulations are likely to be strengthened, modified or totally revised based on developments and information which arise during treatment implementation. As a result, treatment goals and contracts may have to be renegotiated. On the other hand, treatment monitoring and evaluation may take place simultaneously, with early indications of failure leading to changes in treatment implementation. Our purpose in logically distinguishing three phases of practice is to promote an understanding of the different functions and tasks involved in clinical practice rather than to definitively describe it. With these caveats behind us, let us go on to describe the practice tasks and decisions associated with treatment implementation and its monitoring.

TASKS

Treatment implementation requires that the clinical social worker accomplish a number of practice tasks and make a number of decisions. The tasks are as follows:

1. First, role-expectations of the social worker, the client, and any relevant significant others are specified. These expectations should be consistent with the initial diagnostic assessment and treatment formulation. In addition, they should be in compliance with the contractual agreement between the social worker and the client. Once these expectations have been *operationally defined* (that is, stated in measurable terms), they can be used for monitoring worker and client compliance with the treatment contract.

2. Next, treatment procedures are implemented. In principle, these procedures are thought to be the most effective and efficient means for achieving the treatment objectives specified in the diagnostic assessment and treatment formulation stage. In addition, they must be practical, ethical and acceptable to the client. In actual practice situations, however, circumstances in the practice environment may seriously limit the extent to which ideal treatment conditions can be realized. For example, although treatment is likely to work best under conditions of client voluntarism, a social worker employed in a correctional facility cannot ignore the element of coercion that is implied in any treatment contract with an inmate. A child guidance worker, doing therapy with a physically handicapped child, cannot ignore parent desires to keep the child dependent. And, what works in theory may not work in practice. Thus, during treatment implementation the clinical social worker should be sensitive to those factors which may interfere with the successful implementation of treatment plans.

3. Once treatment procedures are implemented, worker, client, and possibly significant others' compliance with the treatment contract is monitored. This is accomplished by the collection of data concerning the extent to which these individuals are living up to the expectations enumerated in the treatment contract. Thus, the social worker may suggest that a couple engage in certain activities such as quiet conversation, relaxation techniques, and the like, before attempting sexual relations. The clinician may instruct the couple to report back at the next session, the number of times compliance did and did not take place. Or, a social worker's performance as a nondirective therapist may be monitored by tape recording the worker's interviews with clients. Standards of appropriate therapeutic intervention and nonintervention will be brought by the social worker's supervisor to an analysis of actual interview behavior. This analysis will serve as the basis for supervisory conferences. Finally, a residential employee of a half-way house for former mental patients may be asked to monitor the treatment-relevant behaviors of a patient resident. Does the patient take medication as directed? Does he participate in activity therapy? and so on.

4. Based on the foregoing analyses of treatment implementation and contractual compliance, judgments are made about whether treatment procedures should be continued, modified, or replaced by other procedures. While attempting to implement group treatment with delinquent boys, for example, a social worker may observe that one group member is so fearful and withdrawn that he does not participate in the group process. The worker may decide to work individually with the youngster to help him reach a point where he can assert himself within the group. Or, he may be assigned to another group which is less aggressive and threatening. The major point here is that diagnostic assessment and treatment formulation is a continuing process which is aided by treatment implementation and monitoring. Though logically distinct, the two phases work hand in glove.

IMPLEMENTATION AND MONITORING DECISIONS

Clinical social workers make many crucial decisions during treatment implementation. These decisions are implied within each of the above-mentioned tasks, but they can be specified by indicating some of the questions which the social worker should ask him/herself during this phase of practice. Since clinical practice is a dynamic process, the questions are interrelated and they are related as well to questions of diagnostic assessment and treatment formulation. Treatment evaluation as well may be contingent on answering these questions. Hence, one cannot evaluate the impact of a given treatment intervention unless one knows that the treatment intervention was faithfully implemented. Some of these questions are as follows:

1. Are the expectations of the client, social worker and significant others clearly specified? Are they stated in understandable and measurable terms?

2. Have treatment procedures been implemented in accordance with professional standards, agency rules and the treatment contract?

3. What barriers to successful implementation exist within the practice situation? Can these be neutralized in any way?

4. To what extent do client, clinician and significant others fulfill their contractual obligations? If they don't, why don't they?

5. Are there reasons to revise the initial diagnostic assessment or treatment formulation based on contractual noncompliance?

6. If treatment should be changed, how should this be done?

RESEARCH CONCEPTS AND TECHNIQUES

As with diagnostic assessment and treatment formulation, the concepts of information validity, reliability and representativeness are central to effective treatment monitoring. In addition, research techniques such as standardized interviewing and systematic observation, which were introduced in the context of diagnostic assessment and treatment formulation, are applicable to treatment monitoring as well.

In the following three chapters, we introduce some other research concepts and techniques and apply them to monitoring treatment interventions. In chapter 6, for example, we discuss content analysis, a research technique for systematically analyzing written documents and other preserved forms of communication such as films, videotapes, and the like. We illustrate the use of content analysis of process records by supervisors to monitor worker performance.

Chapter 7 is devoted to form construction. Clients can be taught to use specially constructed forms to monitor their own, therapeutically relevant, activities. This kind of self-monitoring is particularly useful in providing systematic information about what is happening *between* therapeutic sessions when direct observations by the clinician is not possible.

Chapter 8 concerns techniques of aggregating and analyzing the monitoring data collected in a number of comparable cases. This set of techniques makes generalization possible across cases and across clinicians. Such generalizations can provide important information about the kinds of clients with whom particular techniques are most effective in securing treatment contract compliance.

SELECTED BIBLIOGRAPHY

Compton, Beulah R. and Burt Galaway, eds., *Social Work Processes* (Homewood, Ill.: Dorsey Press, 1975), pp. 312–38.

Eisenberg, Sheldon and Daniel J. Delaney, *The Counseling Process* (2d ed.; Chicago: Rand McNally, 1977), pp. 127–82.

Epstein, Irwin and Tony Tripodi, *Research Techniques for Program Planning, Monitoring, and Evaluation* (New York: Columbia University Press, 1977), pp. 55–58.

Pincus, Allen and Anne Minahan, *Social Work Practice: Model and Method* (Itasca, Ill.: F. E. Peacock, 1973), pp. 162–226.

Glasser, Paul, Rosemary Sarri, and Robert Vinter, eds., *Individual*

Change Through Small Groups (New York: Free Press, 1974), pp. 9–33 and 126–48.

Gottman, John M., and Sandra R. Leiblum, *How To Do Psychotherapy and How to Evaluate It* (New York: Holt, Rinehart and Winston, 1974), pp. 43–100.

Hollis, Florence, *Casework: A Psychosocial Therapy* (New York: Random House, 1964), pp. 204–18.

Levy, Rona L. and Robert D. Carter, "Compliance with Practitioner Instigations," *Social Work* (May 1976), 21(3):188–93.

McLean, Peter D., "Evaluating Community-Based Psychiatric Services" in Park O. Davidson, Frank W. Clark, and Leo A. Hamerlynck, eds., *Evaluation of Behavioral Programs* (Champaign, Ill.: Research Press, 1974), pp. 83–102.

Tripodi, Tony, Phillip Fellin, Irwin Epstein, and Roger Lind, Eds., *Social Workers at Work* (2d ed.; Itasca, Ill.: F. E. Peacock, 1977), pp. 64–71.

6

THE USE OF CONTENT ANALYSIS TO MONITOR SOCIAL WORKER PERFORMANCE

Content analysis is a research procedure for obtaining systematic, quantitative, descriptive information from written documents, films, tape recordings, photographs, and the like. The principles of content analysis are similar to those involved in systematic observation. The major difference between these two research techniques is that content analysis is applied to data already available to the researcher, whereas systematic observation is generally conducted *in vivo*.

Content analysis may be used to analyze and draw inferences from a variety of communication documents routinely available in clinical social work settings. These include verbatim written "process" recordings of interviews with clients or significant others, summary written reports, tape recordings of individual or group counseling sessions, diaries or logs kept by social workers and/or clients, and so on.

In this chapter, we will focus on the use of content analysis in monitoring the extent to which clinical social workers implement treatment in accordance with treatment planning. The major data source considered will be case records, the most commonly available description of worker–client interaction in clinical settings.

CONTENT ANALYSIS AND CLINICAL SOCIAL WORK PRACTICE

Content analytic techniques can be usefully applied to every phase of clinical social work practice. Thus, for example, a social worker might use this technique to identify problematic themes that emerge in the interactions between husband and wife in early interviews that are tape recorded or that are reported verbatim in process records. Similarly, content analysis can be employed during the treatment implementation phase to determine whether the treatment behaviors of social workers are consistent with agency policy or norms of professional practice. Finally, content analysis may be used to evaluate the success of treatment. Thus, by comparing the frequency and intensity of the mention of problematic themes after treatment has terminated with the frequency and intensity of the mention of the same themes prior to treatment, one can assess progress before and after treatment.

As a technique, content analysis is potentially most valuable to clinical supervision. This is because supervisors rarely have direct access to the interactions between clients and the social workers they supervise. As a result, supervisors are usually totally dependent upon process records and supervisory discussions with line social workers for information about worker–client interaction. With experience, many supervisors become remarkably skillful at reading and analyzing process records. Their approach, however, is largely intuitive. The principles of content analysis, applied to process records, could conceiveably make this effort more systematic and enhance the validity and reliability of the inferences drawn from these records of practice.

PRINCIPLES FOR TREATMENT MONITORING BY CONTENT ANALYSIS

1. Specifying Monitoring Standards

Monitoring standards refer to dimensions reflecting expected therapeutic activities, behaviors and content to be exhibited by clinical social workers. These constitute the ideals against which actual worker performance is assessed. Standards may vary from worker to worker. More will be expected from a seasoned worker than from a worker new to the job. Standards may vary from client to client as well. Obviously, this is so because different clients require different treatment plans. Also, standards may vary from time to time, thus, as treatment knowledge increases, norms of practice change.

Irrespective of what the standards are, they should be stated as clearly as possible, they should be adjusted to the individual worker's treatment style and approach, and they should be reflective of content which may importantly affect the implementation of treatment plans. In treatment situations with a particular worker the ideal may be to get the worker to refrain from monopolizing treatment interviews and to become less didactic or directive. With another worker, the ideal may be to talk more and to be more directive in therapeutic sessions.

The more specific the standards, the more easily they are monitored. This is facilitated by treatment planning which is clear and specific. Nevertheless, the particular indicators of these ideal dimensions will emerge from the process recordings themselves. For example, in attempting to monitor how directive a social worker is, the supervisor cannot anticipate the many specific ways in which directiveness may display itself.

2. Specifying Sources of Data and Their Availability

Data for treatment monitoring should be drawn from available documents which adequately reflect worker-client interactions.

Process recordings are usually the best sources of such information. However, even when process recordings are physically available, their availability may not be consistent (Shyne 1975). Ideally, process records should be consistently available over time, across cases, and across workers. If one wanted to monitor treatment of a single case, adequate process recordings of every worker–client interview must be available. If one wanted to compare treatment done by a single worker with clients who required comparable treatment, adequate process records would have to be available for each of these clients. Finally, if one wanted to compare the performance of social workers, they would each have to make available adequate process recordings for comparable clients, over time.

Another aspect of availability is how systematic the process recording is. If one desires to make comparisons of worker activity over time, for example, each interview must be completely described. Otherwise, as treatment proceeds, selective bias may enter into the worker's rendition of what has transpired between the client and him/herself.

When data are not consistently available or unsystematic, treatment monitoring through content analysis requires that social workers begin to record routinely and systematically their practice. This is time-consuming and may understandably be viewed as burdensome. It is, however, the only way in which valid and reliable inferences can be made.

3. Estimating the Authenticity of the Documents Used

Whether one is a spy, content analyzing secret documents, or a social work supervisor analyzing case records, inferences drawn from these documents are only valid to the extent that the documents are valid. In the context of treatment, documents are authentic to the extent that they are representative of what actually transpired in treatment sessions. Naturally then, a film or videotape of an interview is more likely to be authentic than a process record dictated from notes, two weeks after the actual interview has transpired. Since process records are more likely to be available than videotapes, monitoring may necessarily be confined to analysis of the former, written documents. Nevertheless, to promote the greatest possible authenticity, process recording should take place immediately after the interview has transpired and should be based on as copious note-taking as sound therapeutic interviewing will allow.

Another aid to authenticity in process recording involves encouraging workers to be as behaviorally specific as they can be in their descriptions of their client's and their own behavior. Inferences or generalizations such as "the client appeared defensive" should be recognized as such and be backed up by behaviorally specific descriptions of the client behaviors which led to this generalization. Likewise, general statements about social worker activities should go beyond references such as "the worker empathized with the client" to what the worker, in fact, said.

Finally, the content of case recording should be as relevant to treatment planning and as accurate as possible. Sometimes it is possible to check the accuracy of the process record by comparing inferences made from the process record with data collected by other means. Thus, for example, process recording describing therapeutic gains in worker–client interactions in an adolescent treatment institution may be compared with data drawn from interviews with cottage parents, teachers, and so on. Wherever possible, this kind of external validation is encouraged.

4. Defining the Units of Analysis

In the context of content analysis, the unit of analysis refers to the informational units that will be categorized or coded. Identifying the unit of analysis involves specifying the information that the content analyst should pay attention to in developing categories for analysis. The unit of analysis may be as detailed as every word in a document or as broad as whole sections of documents. Sentences, thought units, thematic content areas, and the like can all serve as units of analysis.

Naturally, the more detailed the content analysis, the smaller the unit of analysis. However, the more detailed the analysis, the more time-consuming and expensive it will be. Consequently, the unit of analysis should be small enough so that it provides reliable and valid information pertinent to the purpose of the analysis, but not so small that it requires excessive amounts of time and money for processing and analyzing the data.

5. Operationally Defining Analytic Categories

Once units of analysis have been broadly defined, the materials which are to be content analyzed are perused for the purpose of identifying dimensions of variables that are relevant to the purpose of the study and that are translatable into nominal, ordinal or interval scales. Thus, for example, a therapeutic interview may be looked at in order to determine which type of therapeutic intervention predominates. The therapeutic interview is the unit of analysis, the type of intervention which predominates is the variable which is to be analyzed, and the categories of types of intervention represents a nominal scale whose categories are based upon what emerges from studying a sample of interviews. Likewise, a therapeutic interview might be divided into three fifteen-minute units of analysis. The variable to be analyzed may be type of therapeutic intervention, but it may be represented as an ordinal scale in which each type of intervention within a time unit is ranked in terms of whether it appears most frequently, sometimes, or never. Finally, the unit of analysis may be as detailed as every sentence uttered by the social worker. The variable to be measured may be an interval scale in which the frequency of empathic statements are counted.

Just as in other efforts to operationally define variables, the categories for analysis should be mutually exclusive and exhaustive. In content analysis, however, the categories and their behavioral referents will come primarily from studying the documents to be analyzed themselves rather than from categories that are fully formed before the documents are reviewed. Once these are identified, specific instructions should be written concerning which information to consider and which to ignore, what code categories are to be used and, finally, what are the empirical referents for assigning code categories to units of analysis. Illustrative examples of each code category are helpful as well. The more detailed these instructions, the more reliable the classification scheme.

6. Determining the Reliability of Analytic Categories

The procedures for determining the reliability of measures in content analysis are identical to those described in our chapter on observational techniques (see chapter 4). In content analysis, test-retest and inter-rater reliability are particularly relevant. Test-retest reliability should be established when content analysis of documents is to take place over a long period of time. This will insure the fact that the one or more people who are rating the documents are not changing the bases of their judgments in the course of the study. Inter-rater reliability, on the other hand, is important to establish to insure the fact that different raters are consistent in their judgments of the same materials.

Once the categories for content analysis have been selected, the following guidelines should help to promote the reliability of coding procedures:

1. Make sure the basic dimensions or variables to be identified are clearly defined and understood by the raters.

2. Make sure instructions for categorization of these variables are clear. This is promoted by basing categories on behavioral manifestations that are closely related to the overt content of the documents to be analyzed. Thus, a count of the number of times a client used the word "angry" is likely to be more reliable than a count of the number of times the client "appeared hostile."

3. On a small but varied sample of the documents to be analyzed, have raters make independent ratings on the key dimensions in the study. Calculate the inter-rater reliability on these dimensions. If the reliability is too low (say, below 70 percent agreement), discuss those instances in which there were differences in

judgments. Then refine the rules for categorizing dimensions. Conduct ratings on a second sample to determine whether reliability has been brought to an acceptable level.

4. Once, inter-rater reliability has been established, actual data-collection may begin. However, it is important to establish that the reliability is maintained over the course of the study. Ratings, therefore, should be "spot-checked" against the documents on which they are based throughout the study.

5. Finally, reliability is likely to decline when raters are fatigued, bored or under great time pressure. It is important, therefore, that work schedules and conditions be such that these negative conditions are minimized.

7. *Defining and Securing the Study Materials*

The materials which are to serve as a data source for content analysis can be defined in terms of their sources, dates and contents (Selltiz et al. 1959). The *sources* may be existing process records, other written file materials, tapes, diaries, and so on. If only one source is used, it is important to establish that this source gives an authentic and comprehensive picture of the phenomenon which is to be studied. Thus, for example, a content analysis of an abusing parent's statements about his or her child management practices would be a poor source of data concerning actual parent-child behaviors. When multiple sources are employed, it is important to establish how authentic and comprehensive each of these sources is.

Dates refer to the different times for which materials are available. Where multiple sources are used, there may be different dates for each source. For instance, a school social worker's process records may describe ten interviews with a child, two interviews with the child's parents, and one interview with the child's teacher over the course of a semester. Each of these sources of information may be content analyzed. In the final report of such a study, information regarding the dates and frequency of this material should be provided so that proper interpretations may be made in relation to study findings. One would give more credence to study based on records of weekly interviews over the course of a semester than on a content analysis of a single interview at the end of a semester.

Contents refers to the actual communications data that are to be analyzed for each source, for each date. Here again, it is important that the contents of the materials to be analyzed constitute as authentic a representation of the phenomenon to be studied as possible. A study based entirely on the contents of memos from a social worker to his/her supervisor would be a poor source of information about what transpires between worker and client.

8. Collecting, Tabulating, and Presenting the Data

Sometimes data sources for content analysis are voluminous. Under these circumstances it would be too time-consuming and costly to study *all* relevant documents. At these times a sample of the total set of documents is selected (procedures for sampling are discussed in chapter 9). Once the study materials have been collected, raters should be meticulous in recording and counting data. Spot checks of reliability will also reveal inaccuracies and sloppiness in recording. Awareness of the spot checks themselves keeps raters alert and promotes accuracy.

After recording and tabulating the data, results should be presented in a form that is easy to read and relevant to the purpose of the analysis. Since many of the findings of content analyses are in the forms of simple counts or percentages, simple bar graphs and line graphs are quite useful for presenting study findings. Thus, for example, Hans Strupp (1966) effectively employed bar graphs to represent changes in therapeutic activity over time.

In a bar graph, the bars may be either horizontal or vertical. The area within each bar represents 100 percent of a particular dimension, for example, total time involved in a therapeutic interview. Within the bar, different symbols can be used to represent different categories and their relative frequency within a given dimension. For example, in monitoring changes in client–worker interaction over time, a bar may represent each interview. Within each bar, a blank space may represent the relative amount of silence, a diagonally striped space may represent the relative amount of time the therapist spoke and a dotted space may represent the amount of client talk time. By constructing the bar graph for each recorded interview and placing them side by side, one can easily discern changes over time.

Figure 6.1 shows that there has been a sizable reduction in therapist talk time over the course of four interviews and a corresponding increase in client talking. In addition, the periods of silence have declined.

The same findings may be represented in a line graph (figure 6.2), in which the percent of interview time is represented on the vertical axis, the interviews on the horizontal axis, and the different data categories by separate symbolic lines.

It should be clear from figures 6.1 and 6.2 that the bar graph is better for representing *relative* amounts of each category of worker-client communication, whereas the line graph is better for representing *absolute* amounts of each category. Each, however, offers the findings in a manner which is easy to read and interpret.

9. Comparing Findings Against Monitoring Standards

The final step in any treatment monitoring study involves comparing the findings against standards for worker performance. These standards may be derived empirically, that is, based on the performance of other workers. They may be based on agency rules, professional norms, or specific treatment plans. Whatever their origin, guidelines should be established for determining what constitutes a serious departure from the standard of acceptable worker performance. This is often a matter of judgment based on previous experience and taking into account such considerations as the level of worker training and experience, the severity of clinical impairment of the client, and the like. If serious discrepancies are noted between actual worker performance and standards, the documentation of these discrepancies can serve as a useful tool for supervisory intervention.

FIGURE 6.1

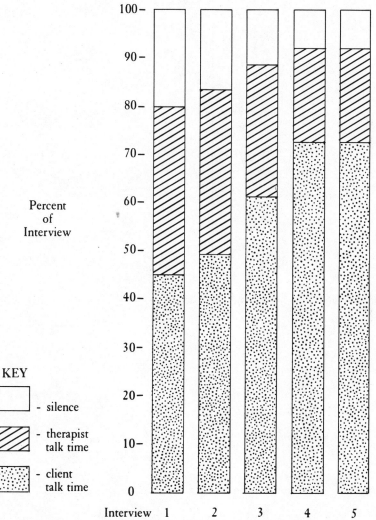

FIGURE 6.2

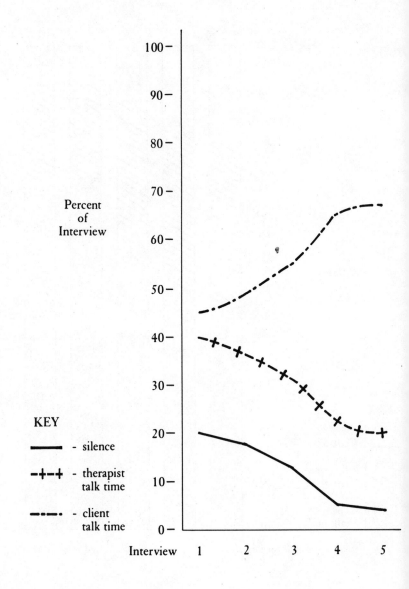

HYPOTHETICAL ILLUSTRATION

A supervisor of a student unit in a community mental health center discovers that one of her four students was having difficulty getting clients to return for service after the first two interviews. The clinic was located in a public housing project and served a low-income clientele. The program offered short-term supportive treatment accompanied by assistance with money management, medical, employment referrals, and the like. In supervisory conferences the student appears intelligent and perceptive and seems to accept instruction readily. The supervisor decides to do a content analysis of the process records in an attempt to locate the problem.

1. Specifying Monitoring Standards

The general standard for treatment in this unit is short-term treatment geared to altering the client's situation through referral, advice-giving, advocacy, and emotional support.

2. Specifying Sources of Data and Their Availability

The supervisor decides to do a content analysis of the process records of all of the students in the unit. Students are required to provide extensive process recording on all of their cases. She instructs all students to bring their process recording up to date. Once these are available, she can compare the performance of the student in question with other students.

3. Estimating the Authenticity of the Documents Used

Since students have been instructed to complete their process recordings immediately after their interviews with clients, she assumes that the records are fairly authentic representations of what the students remember of the interviews. She has also encouraged students to be as specific as possible in describing worker–client interactions. By comparing student interpretations of client-behavior with their descriptions she can get a sense of the authenticity of the students' rendition of what has transpired and why. Naturally, an additional outside source of information will be the rate of client return. A process record describing a high level of client involvement that is followed by nonreturn raises questions about the authenticity of the document.

4. Defining the Units of Analysis

The supervisor decides that each recorded interview will constitute a unit of analysis. Since each student has had approximately five cases, and each of these has had from one to four interviews, the total number of interviews is small enough to not require sampling procedures.

5. Operationally Defining Analytic Categories

The supervisor determines that she wants to compare the treatment activities of each student social worker in their recorded interviews. Taking a single interview from each student, she peruses the records to get a general sense of kinds of student-initiated behaviors revealed in these records. Four kinds of student-initiated behaviors immediately become apparent. They are asking questions, giving direct advice, making empathic statements, and making interpretive statements. She then goes back to the records to identify the behavioral bases for her intuitive judgments about these dimensions. These will serve as guides for subsequent analysis of all the process records. Questions are easily discernible in the process records where students indicate that they asked the client something. Advice-giving statements are those in which the student indicates that s/he offered instruction to the client, told the client what to do, and so on. Empathic statements are those in which the student expresses compassion and understanding of the client's situation and feelings. Interpretive statements are those in which the student attempts to explain the client's attitudes, feelings, or behaviors based on previous information which the client has volunteered.

By simply counting the number of times each student takes each of these actions, and dividing by the total number of actions that the student has recorded, one can get a relative picture of the differences among students on each of these dimensions.

6. Determining the Reliability of Analytic Categories

Since the supervisor is the only one that will be rating student behaviors, she is concerned only with intra-rater reliability, that is the extent to which her ratings are internally consistent. After coding the first four interviews, she records them to determine that her ratings are consistent. There is a high level of agreement in her ratings for each of the student-initiated activities.

7. Defining and Securing the Study Materials

It has already been determined that the study will be based on all of the student unit's process recording. The supervisor collects all of these and notes which records come from which students, as well as the relationship between the date each interview took place and the date of process recording. This provides further confirmation of the authenticity of the records.

8. Collecting, Tabulating, and Presenting the Data

The supervisor proceeds to tally the number of times each student indicates that s/he asked a question, gave advice, demonstrated empathy, and made interpretive statements. By dividing by the total number of student-initiated statements in the process recording of a given student, she can easily convert these findings into percentages and display them in a bar graph. Figure 6.3 shows the relative proportion of each of these types of student-initiated activity for each student.

9. Comparing Findings with Monitoring Standards.

Figure 6.3 shows that Student D, the one who was having difficulty getting clients to return, is lowest in advice-giving and empathetic statements and highest in asking questions and in providing interpretation to the client. This high level of interpretive

FIGURE 6.3

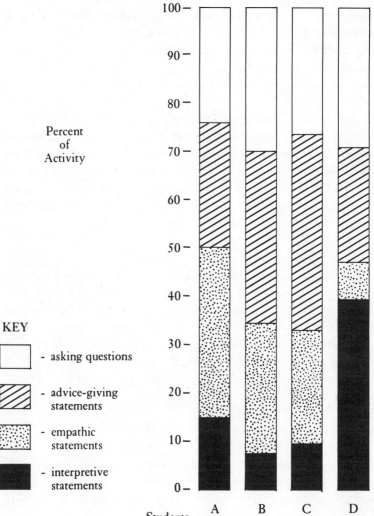

activity and relatively low level of empathy and direct advice-giving is also inconsistent with treatment standards of the agency as a whole.

Using the bar graph for illustrative purposes, the supervisor discusses these findings with the student, who acknowledges that s/he would prefer to be doing long-term, nondirective psychotherapy with clients. Having identified the problem through systematic monitoring of the student behavior with clients, the supervisor can proceed to work with the student on this issue.

EXERCISE

Select a transcript of one therapeutic interview from your own or someone else's clinical practice. Identify three types of worker activity. Divide the interview into three parts—beginning, middle, and end. What is the incidence of each of the three types of worker activity within each segment of the interview? Does the incidence of each of these activities change from segment to segment?

SELECTED BIBLIOGRAPHY

Berelson, Bernard, "Content Analysis," in Gardiner Lindzey, ed., *Handbook of Social Psychology* (Reading, Mass.: Addison-Wesley, 1954), pp. 488–522.

Best, John W., *Research in Education* (2d ed. Englewood Cliffs, N.J.: Prentice-Hall, 1970), pp. 133–34.

Blalock, Hubert M., *Social Statistics* (New York: McGraw-Hill, 1960), pp. 437–40.

Labov, William and David Fanshel, *Therapeutic Discourse: Psychotherapy as Conversation* (New York: Academic Press, 1977), pp. 1–30.

Marsden, Gerald, "Content Analysis Studies of Therapeutic Interviews: 1954 to 1964," in Gary E. Stallak, Bernard G. Guerney, Jr., and Meyer Rothberg, eds., *Psychotherapy Research* (Chicago: Rand McNally, 1966), pp. 336–64.

Selltiz, Claire, Marie Jahoda, Morton Deutsch, and Stuart W. Cook, *Research Methods in Social Relations* (rev. ed.; New York: Holt, 1959), pp. 335–42.

Shyne, Ann W., "Exploiting Available Information" in Norman A. Polansky, ed., *Social Work Research* (rev. ed.; Chicago: University of Chicago Press, 1975), pp. 109–30.

Strupp, Hans H., "A Multidimensional Comparison of Therapist Activity in Analytic and Client-Centered Therapy," in Gary E. Stallak, Bernard G. Guerney, Jr., and Meyer Rothberg, eds., *Psychotherapy Research* (Chicago: Rand McNally, 1966), pp. 430–39.

7

THE USE OF FORMS FOR CLIENT SELF-MONITORING

In this age of accountability, third-party payments, and the like, forms often are viewed negatively by social work clinicians. More likely than not, they are seen as a waste of time and as a detractor from direct service with clients. When designed and used properly, however, forms can be highly efficient devices for generating systematic, objective, treatment-relevant information about clients. This information can come from client self-monitoring forms or from client monitoring forms completed by significant others.

Client monitoring forms are particularly useful in "open settings" such as family service agencies, child guidance clinics, community mental health agencies, etc., where the client is treated intermittently and observed only in interaction with the social worker. In such settings, the client's subjective recollections are generally the primary source of information concerning client problems, efforts to deal with these and success or failure in resolving them.

For improving the quality of client self-reporting, forms can be used for systematically and routinely recording client behaviors, attitudes, and moods. Moreover, they are especially useful in gathering information about client compliance with the treatment contract. In this chapter, we show how client self-monitoring forms can be used to assess the quantity and quality of the client's adherence to worker directives.

So, rather than viewing forms as a vestige of bureaucracy, we believe that when appropriately used, they can streamline and improve the information-gathering process in clinical practice. One final point. Although the construction of forms is not, strictly speaking, a "research technique," good forms make use of concepts and principles that are basic to all research instruments. Thus, concepts and principles for constructing observation instruments, questionnaires, rating scales, and other research instruments are relevant to form construction. What differentiates forms from these other techniques, is that forms are used routinely and with greater frequency. In practice, however, this distinction fades. Consequently, the reader is referred to other chapters in this book as well to obtain a more comprehensive picture of the potentials and requisites of good forms.

CLIENT SELF-MONITORING FORMS AND CLINICAL PRACTICE

Client self-monitoring forms are potentially useful in all phases of clinical social work practice. In the diagnostic assessment phase, for example, they can be used to "baseline" the occurence of problematic behaviors, attitudes or moods at regular intervals prior to intervention. Such systematic monitoring of problems and the contingencies that effect their expression can greatly aid clinical diagnosis.

Forms also can be used to systematically assess treatment outcomes. Thus, a series of post-intervention measures taken by the client him/herself or by significant others can determine the effects of treatment and the persistence of these effects. Interrupted time series designs (see chapter 11) make use of both pre- and post-intervention measures in evaluating clinical outcomes.

Finally, forms can be used to determine how faithfully the client is following treatment directives. Again, this monitoring can be done by clients themselves and/or by significant others in their environment. What's important is that the information generated in this monitoring process is part of a regular, systematic and objective effort to describe client behavior.

PRINCIPLES FOR DEVELOPING AND USING FORMS

1. Determining the Purpose of the Form

In considering the potential usefulness of a client self-monitoring form, it is important to consider two questions. First, what kind of information is sought? In the context of treatment implementation, three different kinds of information can be secured through the use of client self-monitoring forms: (1) information concerning client adherence to treatment procedures and/or time schedules which have been agreed to in a verbal or written contract with the social worker; (2) information concerning situational factors which facilitate or obstruct client compliance; and (3) information concerning client behaviors, attitudes, or moods during the treatment process.

Thus, for example, forms can be used to determine the frequency with which a client in a job counseling program contacts potential employers, the conditions under which the client does so, and his/her self-attitudes following these contacts. Likewise, a parent in a child-abuse prevention program can be asked to record the frequency with which s/he uses physical punishment versus alternative means, the factors which precipitated the use of physical punishment, and the client's self-attitudes following these events.

A second question to ask when considering a client monitoring form is whether the desired information is already available through some other, less obtrusive means. If the client, for example, appears to have sufficient insight, distance, and objectivity to reliably report this information, a form may not be necessary. Alternatively, a form may be unnecessary when the information can be secured from significant others who can provide reliable and valid information based on existing "natural" or research devices. Specifying the informational purpose of the form, however, helps determine whether the information is already available through other means.

2. Setting Treatment Monitoring Standards

One cannot adequately monitor treatment implementation without first specifying expectations or standards of social worker and client behavior. Whether monitoring worker or client, the more specific the standards, the easier the monitoring. For example, an overweight client may be asked to "keep track of his/her weight" during a one-week period. This lack of specificity will probably result in sporadic, self-monitoring efforts on the part of the client and unreliable information for the clinician. On the other hand, a client asked to weigh him/herself daily, at the same time, unclothed, and to record the weight on a simple weekly form will produce much more reliable information. Moreover, the information will not only indicate the success or failure of weight-reduction efforts; the client's compliance with the self-monitoring instructions also represents a measure of the client's commitment to and compliance with treatment.

Just as with treatment expectations, monitoring expectations should be as specific as possible. How often is the form to be filled out? Under what conditions? When are the forms to be returned to the social worker? Questions like these should be clearly answered in the monitoring instructions.

3. Determining Who Fills Out the Form

In this chapter, we are emphasizing client self-monitoring. However, the person(s) who uses the form may be anyone who regularly observes the client's treatment-relevant behaviors. It may be a relative, friend, nurse, teacher, co-worker, employer, and so on. When client self-monitoring is the primary source of information, any of the above may be used to determine the reliability of the client's self-reports. Such external checks are particularly useful when there is reason to think that the client's self-reports might be biased.

In deciding who should use the form, it is important to consider who can follow the monitoring instructions and respond in a reliable, unbiased manner. Naturally, for forms to be used, a minimum degree of literacy is necessary. Instructions must be understandable and geared to the user's level of knowledge and sophistication.

4. Constructing Treatment Monitoring Forms

In many respects, the principles that apply to the construction of interview schedules (see chapter 2) and follow-up questionnaires (see chapter 9) are equally applicable to the construction of treatment monitoring forms. Information should be operationally specific, valid, and reliable. Categories within an informational dimension should be mutually exclusive and exhaustive. Each question should relate to a single category of information about client behavior, attitude, mood, and/or the conditions affecting these.

The information generated may be *quantitative* numerical counts of client behaviors, ratings of client attitudes or moods, and so on. Or, information may be *qualitative*, based on narrative descriptions of client behaviors and the conditions affecting these. The former are appropriate when the standards of treatment-relevant behaviors are highly specified. The latter are most useful when standards lack specificity. In the course of treatment, the clinician may begin with qualitative monitoring and, based upon this, develop more specific standards and a more quantitative form. Or, a form may have a combination of qualitative and quantitative questions. In general, simple adherence to social worker directives should be registered in simple quantitative categories of one kind or another. Questions about problems in following treatment directives should be answered qualitatively, providing ideas about obstacles to treatment that the worker did not anticipate.

Whether quantitative, qualitative or a mixture of both, treatment monitoring forms should be constructed with the following principles in mind:

a. The information gathered by the form should have a basic relation to treatment monitoring objectives. In other words, the information gathered should reflect directly on issues of client adherence to the treatment contract and/or factors which facilitate or obstruct adherence.

b. Each form should contain sufficient identifying information so that if it is misplaced it can be traced back to particular clients. This is especially important if similar monitoring forms are used in a number of agency cases.

c. Each form should indicate the dates on which the monitoring took place. This will make it possible to analyze client compliance over time.

d. Duplication of information should be avoided. Beyond the minimum essentials, information which is already available in agency records should not be requested on monitoring forms. If, in the future, an attempt is made to correlate client compliance with other client characteristics, the latter information can be retrieved easily enough from the case records.

e. For each category of information, a precise operational definition or set of instructions should be given to facilitate classification and tabulation of the data and to promote validity and reliability of the data.

f. Operational definitions should be consistent on all forms given to a single client. If a number of clients are engaged in similar treatment efforts, operational definitions should be consistent in the forms given to each of these clients. This is particularly important if the client data are to be combined (see chapter 8) to make generalizations about over-all client compliance within the program as a whole.

g. Forms should be simple, clear, efficient, and easy to use. When they are complicated or time-consuming they result in fatigue and unreliability. Ideally, a client self-monitoring form should not require more than ten minutes to complete.

h. Where possible, validating procedures should be built into the monitoring efforts. The social worker should discuss the results of the monitoring regularly with the client who is monitoring his/her own compliance. In addition, significant others in the client's environment may be asked to validate the client's self-monitoring.

i. When qualitative descriptions are called for, instructions for

recording these should be as specific as possible. If "critical incidents" are to be described, definitions and examples should be
provided as well as instructions for how much information needs
to be provided.

5. Pretesting the Form

Before using the form for systematic data collection, it should be
tried out. The social worker should first discuss the form with the
client, giving instructions and providing examples to illustrate how
it should be used. Between treatment sessions, the client will be
asked to fill out the form and to consider ambiguities in the instructions, how much time it took, whether it was fatiguing, whether
important questions or answer categories were left out, and so on.
The experience of the pretest and the quality of the information re-
treived then should be used by the social worker to make up a final
version of the form to be used in systematically monitoring client
compliance.

6. Collecting the Data

To insure the collection of accurate, high-quality information,
procedures should be worked out so that the client records his/her
behaviors, attitudes, moods and so on, at regular intervals during
the day or at the end of each day. In the case of multiple recordings
in a day, the form should be kept in an easily accessible place to facilitate using it. For those forms which are filled out at the end of
the day, the client should be encouraged to follow that instruction
rather than to let it go until the next day. Leaving it to the next day
promotes unreliable information.

Whatever the timing, client self-monitors should be praised and
rewarded for completing the forms, for providing accurate information, for writing clearly, and so on.

7. Analyzing the Data

At regular intervals, say every two weeks, the social worker and
client should analyze the data collected together. This process

should begin with noting obvious inaccuracies, gaps, mistakes, or inconsistencies in the data recorded. When these are located, they should be clarified.

Once it is established that the information gathered is accurate and complete, the findings are tabulated (see chapter 8) and compared against the client expectations specified in the treatment contract. Is the client faithfully following the social workers instructions? If not, why not? If s/he is, are there indications of a positive change with regard to the treatment objectives? If this appears to be so, treatment and monitoring will continue. If not, a new round of diagnostic assessment and treatment formulation may be called for.

Naturally, no precise formula can be given for answering the questions and making the decisions described in the foregoing paragraph. This is an area in which judgments must be made about whether discrepancies between ideal client behavior and actual client behavior are within tolerable limits. Here, there is no substitute for practice wisdom based on clinical experience. It is our contention, however, that systematic monitoring of client compliance can facilitate this judgment process. And, it may have beneficial treatment effects as well by giving the client a more concrete role in the treatment process.

HYPOTHETICAL ILLUSTRATION

A married couple is in conjoint therapy. The problem that brought them into treatment was that the husband was spending more and more time out of the house, drinking with friends, while the wife became more and more depressed. After some initial diagnostic interviews with the couple, the social worker felt that there was a dual problem. First, since the couple's children had grown and left the house, the woman was suffering from depression commonly referred to as "empty nest syndrome." Many of her functions as a mother were no longer required. The rewards as well as the obligations attached to this role were absent and missed. As a result, the woman became more dependent on her husband for social and pyschological support, activity and the like. This led to conflicts about how to spend their time in the evenings and on weekends.

The social worker determined that two courses of treatment should be undertaken. In individual sessions with the wife, s/he helps explore potential job skills and interests and encourages the woman to seek employment during the day. In conjoint sessions, s/he teaches husband and wife techniques of negotiation and conflict resolution. No direct effort is made to limit the time the husband spends outside the home. Both husband and wife agree to participate in self-monitoring during the course of treatment. For monitoring purposes, two forms will be constructed, one for the husband and one for the wife.

1. Determining the Purpose of the Form

The forms are intended to serve a number or purposes. They are to monitor (1) the woman's efforts to find outside employment, (2) the incidence of marital conflict between the couple, (3) the use of negotiation techniques taught by the social worker, (4) the woman's feelings of depression, and (5) the frequency with which the couple go out socially together or separately.

2. Setting Treatment Monitoring Standards

It is determined that the forms should be filled out daily. Husband and wife are asked to fill out their forms separately, without consultation with each other. The wife is instructed to complete the job-seeking activities section each day before starting dinner. Both are instructed to complete the remaining items before going to bed.

3. Determining Who Fills Out the Form

Both husband and wife will each have their own form to fill out. Her form will require information about her job-seeking activities, as well as about the incidence of marital conflict, the use of negotiation techniques, and so on. His form will have questions about everything but her job-seeking activities. By having each fill out a separate form, without consultation with each other, it will be possible to assess the reliability of their self-monitoring.

4. Constructing Treatment Monitoring Forms

The forms will combine quantitative and qualitative questions. Quantitative questions will be asked to record simple factual data such as the number of job inquiries made in a day. Qualitative questions will be asked about the issues over which the couple came into conflict and the conditions under which negotiation techniques did not seem to work.

The wife's form would look something like this:

Name _____ Day _____ Date _____

Job-Seeking Activities
  1. Read wants ads   yes ____ no ____
  2. Number of telephone inquiries made ____
  3. Number of appointments made for job interviews ____
  4. Number of job interviews ____
  5. Other related job seeking activity _____
     _____
     _____

Marital Conflicts

List each issue over which you came into conflict today.	Were negotiation techniques used?		Did they help?	
	Yes	*No*	*Yes*	*No*
1. _____				
2. _____				
3. _____				
4. _____				
5. _____				
6. _____				
7. _____				

Wife's Mood
Which of the following best describes the way you felt today? (check one)

Very   Moderately   Neither happy
happy ____   happy ____   nor depressed ____
Moderately   Very
depressed ____   depressed ____

Social Activities
Did you engage in any social activities today?
    yes ____ no ____
If yes were they with or without your husband?
    With husband ____ Without husband ____

5. Pretesting the Form

Before fully implementing the self-monitoring, the social worker explains the purpose of the form and gives instructions to the couple on how to record information relevant to the conflict section of the form. When both seem to understand the purpose, how to complete the form, and express willingness to do so, they are asked to try it out for a day or two. Their experience with this pretesting will be discussed at their next session and ambiguities will be clarified, questions changed, or instructions given, as necessary.

6. Collecting the Data

Husband and wife have been relatively compliant in completing the forms during the first week of self-monitoring. The social worker praises both for their effort and their obvious commitment to making the most out of their involvement in the therapeutic process.

7. Analyzing the Data

By looking at the data the social worker determines that the woman has done little, during the first week of monitoring, beyond occasional looking at the want ads. This will be pursued further in individual sessions with the wife. The information regarding marital conflicts indicates that both husband and wife show a fairly high level of agreement about the number of conflicts and the issues over which they conflicted. On a few occasions, negotiation techniques were successfully used. On others, though the techniques failed, information about why they failed generated content for further discussion and clarification of the techniques of negotiation. There was further indication that on a few days, the wife indicated that she was neither happy nor depressed and that on one occasion both she and her husband engaged in social activities together. All these factors were taken as positive signs by the social worker. As a result, both treatment and treatment monitoring are continued.

EXERCISE

Devise a form to monitor some specific treatment directives which you give one of your clients. Ask the client to monitor his/her own treatment relevant behavior for a week. To what extent are the data obtained from the forms useful to you? Do the data generated by the form coincide with what the client tells you verbally about the preceding week? Do they coincide with information gathered from significant others in the client's environment?

SELECTED BIBLIOGRAPHY

Epstein, Irwin and Tony Tripodi, *Research Techniques for Program Planning, Monitoring, and Evaluation* (New York: Columbia University Press, 1977), pp. 59–81.

Gottman, John M. and Sandra R. Leiblum, *How To Do Psychotherapy and How To Evaluate It* (New York: Holt, Rinehart and Winston, 1974), pp. 56–58.

Hersen, Michel and David H. Barlow, *Single Case Experimental Designs* (New York: Pergamon Press, 1976), pp. 131–38.

Selltiz, Claire, and Marie Johoda, Morton Deutsch, and Stuart W. Cook, *Research Methods in Social Relations* (rev. ed.; New York: Holt, 1959), pp. 402–406.

Shyne, Ann W., "Exploiting Available Information," in Norman

A. Polansky, ed., *Social Work Research* (revised ed.; Chicago: University of Chicago Press, 1975), pp. 109–30.

Terry, George R., *Principles of Management* (6th ed.; Homewood, Ill.: Richard D. Irwin, 1972), pp. 549–610.

8

THE USE OF
DATA AGGREGATION AND
ANALYSIS FOR TREATMENT
MONITORING

If treatment data are to be useful in clinical practice, they must be analyzed properly. Procedures for doing so involve techniques for aggregating, summarizing, manipulating, analyzing, and interpreting data economically and in such a way that appropriate inferences can be drawn from findings. These inferences may be based on an aggregated data set describing the ongoing treatment of a single client. Alternatively, inferences may be based on aggregated data describing the treatment of a number of comparable clients receiving comparable treatment. In the first instance, generalizations are made about a single client. In the second, generalizations are made about a "class" or set of comparable clients. In either case, data-analytic procedures rely on relatively simple concepts from statistics, measurement theory, and information processing.

In this chapter, some research concepts and techniques derived from the foregoing areas are applied to the processing of data concerning treatment compliance. More specifically, the chapter attempts to demonstrate how techniques of aggregation and data analysis can be applied to information about individual client's compliance or a class of clients' compliance with treatment contracts.

Three sets of procedures are presented: first, the use of whole numbers, averages, and dispersions; second, the use of proportions; and third, the use of cross-tabulations. For each, a set of principles is articulated, and examples are presented. Finally, a simple but widely used statistic is introduced—the chi-square. In the context of this chapter, it is used to determine whether clients receiving one type of treatment recommendation at intake are significantly more likely to return for treatment than are clients receiving another treatment recommendation.

DATA AGGREGATION, ANALYSIS, AND CLINICAL PRACTICE

Data aggregation and analysis are essential to all types of research and useful in all phases of clinical social work practice. In diagnosis and treatment planning, for example, the social worker may need to make diagnostic inferences about a client based on a number of clinical observations. Only by properly aggregating and summarizing these observations can appropriate diagnostic inferences be made. In treatment monitoring, more than likely, compliance data about client or worker involve sets of client or worker behaviors rather than single instances of compliance or noncompliance. These sets of behaviors must be properly accumulated and analyzed to make appropriate generalizations about compliance or noncompliance.

Finally, data-analytic techniques are useful in evaluating treatment outcomes. Thus, in assessing the success of treatment with a single client, the social worker may need to draw inferences from a series of clinical observations. Likewise, in assessing the effectiveness of a type of treatment with a number of clients, outcome information about these clients must be systematically and accurately aggregated and analyzed.

PRINCIPLES FOR USING WHOLE NUMBERS, AVERAGES, AND DISPERSIONS

1. Computing a Frequency Distribution

The simplest kind of data available to a clinician and/or a researcher is the frequency of acts, observations, or individuals falling within each category of a single variable or dimension. If, for example, the job-seeking wife described in the preceding chapter was asked to keep a daily record of the number of telephone inquiries she made about possible jobs, the social worker could aggregate and record this information in the form of a *simple frequency distribution* which would look something like this:

Date	Number of Inquiries
May 1	0
2	2
3	1
4	0
5	1
6	0
7	0
8	2
9	3
10	1
11	3
.	.
.	.
.	.

Total Number of Inquiries = N

If the number of inquiries each day varied considerably, and if treatment lasted for several weeks, a simple frequency distribution might be too cumbersome to compile. In addition, trends in the data might be difficult to perceive. In such instances, the data can be aggregated and analyzed in the form of a *grouped frequency dis-*

tribution based on the number of job inquiries made each week. The weekly frequency distribution might look something like this:

Week	Number of Inquiries
1	4
2	10
3	12
4	5
.	.
.	.

Total Number of Inquiries = N

These findings could be presented more dramatically by converting them into *simple graphs, bar graphs,* or *frequency polygons.* This manner of presentation frequently helps the person viewing the data visualize trends which may be less apparent in the form of whole numbers. In a simple graph, bar graph, or frequency polygon, daily or weekly intervals are plotted along a horizontal axis, with the frequency of inquiry plotted along a vertical axis. In the simple graph (figure 8.1), each day in treatment is represented by a single unit on the horizontal axis. The number of job inquiries each day are represented along the vertical axis and the coordinates of these points are connected with a straight line.

For purposes of presentation, grouped frequency distributions can be converted easily into bar graphs or frequency polygons. In both, weekly intervals are plotted along a horizontal axis, with frequency of job inquiries plotted along a vertical axis. In the bar graph (figure 8.2) the width of each bar corresponds to a weekly interval, and the height of each bar indicates the number of job inquiries made within that interval.

In the frequency polygon (figure 8.3), the number of job inquiries are plotted along the vertical axis at the midpoint of each weekly interval. The points are then connected with straight lines to give a graphic representation of the grouped frequency distribution.

FIGURE 8.1

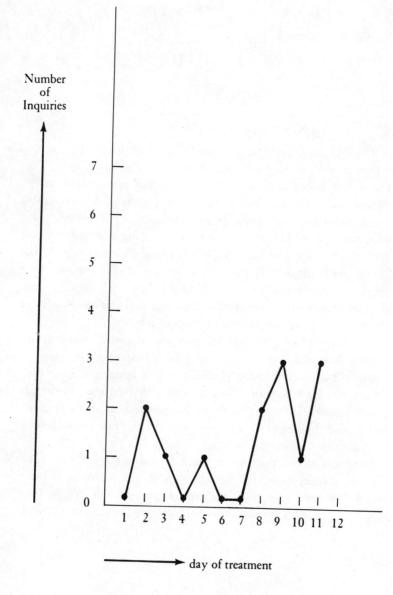

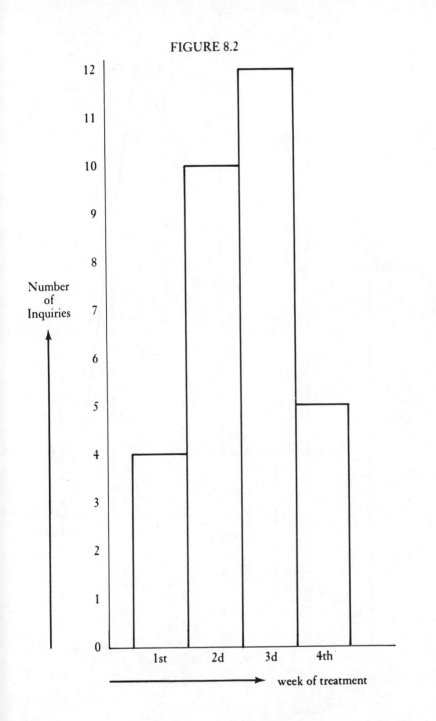

FIGURE 8.2

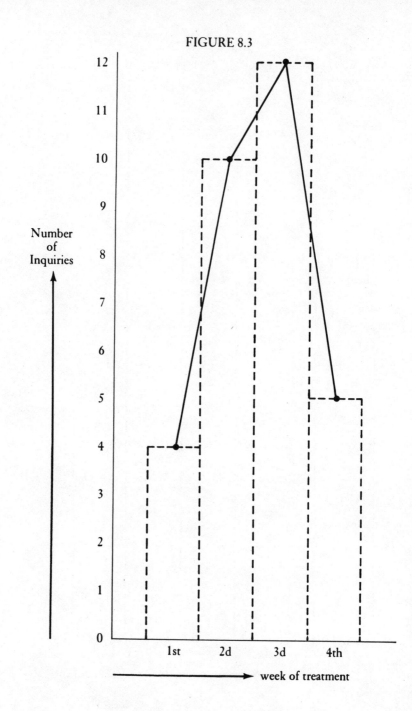

FIGURE 8.3

Grouped frequency data that are graphically presented can reveal patterns which are not apparent when the data are not aggregated. For example, figure 8.1 suggests no clear pattern in daily inquiries; whereas figure 8.3 reveals an increasing number of inquiries until the end of the third week of treatment, after which there is a sharp decline in inquiries. Whether this pattern is unique to this particular client or is common to many clients receiving this form of intervention can only be discerned by aggregating other data based on a number of comparable cases.

2. *Choosing a Measure of Central Tendency*

Once a frequency distribution has been specified, the data contained within can be conveniently summarized in the form of a measure of *central tendency*, or, in more common parlance, an average. These summary measures are useful when there are a great many measurements taken on single variables for individual clients or when data drawn from individual cases are aggregated in order to determine the pattern for all clients receiving comparable treatment.

Social researchers make use of three different measures of central tendency: the arithmetic mean, the median, and the mode. Each has its own advantages and disadvantages. Each offers a way to make an efficient summary statement about the data contained within the frequency distribution.

The *arithmetic mean* $(\overline{X})$ or the arithmetic average is the most widely used measure of central tendency. It is computed from the frequency distribution by taking the frequency within a chosen interval, multiplying it by the value assigned to that interval, and dividing by the total number of units, observations or individuals. Thus, for example, if we wanted to know the mean number of job inquiries made during the first week of treatment by all those clients receiving a comparable form of intervention, we would begin by computing the frequency distribution during the first week for these clients. The distribution might look something like this:

Number of Inquiries	Number of Clients	Inquiries × Clients
0	3	0
1	2	2
2	1	2
3	5	15
4	6	24
5	2	10
.	.	.
.	.	.
.	.	.
20	1	20
	Total = 20	Total = 73

$$\overline{X} = \frac{73}{20}$$
$$\overline{X} = 3.65$$

Taking the sum of the number of inquiries made within the first week of treatment, multiplied by the number of clients making those inquiries (73) and dividing by the total number of clients (20) we arrive at the mean number of inquiries made within the first week of treatment (3.65). By following this procedure for each week of treatment one can derive an average pattern for all clients over the course of their treatment. This could be then plotted on a simple or bar graph for purposes of presentation.

Although the arithmetic mean is widely used and does give the most common interpretation of the "average," it is likely to be distorted or skewed by extreme individual cases in the frequency distribution. Thus, if the last client listed made three instead of twenty inquiries, the mean number of inquiries for the first week would be only 2.8. Clearly then, extreme scores can create a false impression of what the "average" client is likely to do in the first week of treatment.

A second measure of central tendency is the median. The *median* is the point in the distribution that has the same number of scores (as close as possible to 50 percent) above and below it. In the preceding example, the median number of job inquiries for the first week is three. Note that this category leaves six clients below the median and nine above. Clearly, it is less precise than the mean. The advantage of the median, however, is that it is easier to compute. In addition, it is not affected by extreme values the way the mean is. Thus, the median would still be three whether the last client listed made three, twenty, or sixty job inquiries. As a result, the median gives a truer picture of the central tendency in frequency distributions that contain extreme scores. One consequence of this quality is that the median is frequently used in table construction for dividing populations into low and high categories along a given dimension.

A third measure of central tendency is the *mode*. It is the category in the frequency distribution that has the greatest number of scores. It is easiest to compute and least precise. Like the median, however, it is unaffected by extreme scores. In the foregoing example, the mode is four inquiries, since that is the category in which the greatest number of clients fall. In that sense, the most "typical" client makes four job inquiries during the first week of treatment. Note however, that each measure of central tendency has given us a different score based on the same frequency distribution.

3. Dispersions

In studies in which measures of central tendency are used, information about the measures is frequently supplemented with information about the *dispersion* of the frequency distributions. This gives the reader a sense of the shape of the distribution and the degree to which they are skewed or distorted by extreme cases. Two common measures of dispersion are the range and the standard deviation. The *range* is simply the difference between the highest and lowest scores in the distribution. In the foregoing example, the range in number of inquiries made is 20.

The *standard deviation*, on the other hand, indicates the extent to which scores in the distribution cluster around the mean or are highly dispersed. The higher the standard deviation, the greater the dispersion from the mean.*

Whole numbers, averages, and dispersions are also useful for describing relationships between two or more variables. For example, one could describe the relationship between the level of education of the clients in the foregoing example and the number of job inquiries they make by indicating the mean number of inquiries made by women with or without a college education. To do this, one would plot the frequency distribution for each educational grouping. From the two frequency distributions, two means would be computed. This would make comparisons possible between women with lower or higher levels of education.† To determine whether the two distributions are skewed, measures of dispersion would be computed for each group as well.

PRINCIPLES FOR USING PROPORTIONS AND CROSS-TABULATIONS

1. Analyzing Proportions and Their Numerical Bases

The most common forms of data presentation are whole numbers and proportions. Each of these, *taken by itself*, can be extremely misleading. For example, two agencies may represent themselves as providing treatment to clients of all social class groupings. One agency, a relatively small one, indicates that roughly 50 percent of its treatment cases are from low-income families. The other agency, a very large one, reports that it served nearly 100 low-income families in the last year. Only by converting both agencies' service statistics into percentages and determining

---

*For information about the computation of the standard deviation, consult any basic statistics text.

†To determine the statistical significance of the differences between the two mean scores, a statistical test called the *t-test* may be employed. Instructions for computing t-tests may be found in standard texts on statistical methods.

the comparability of the bases on which they were percentaged can one make an apt comparison of the two agencies.

The point of this discussion is that in presenting agency or client data, *the proportions as well as the numbers upon which they were based should be clearly indicated.*

2. Analyzing Cross-Tabulations and the Chi-Square

Cross-tabulations are simple devices for analyzing and presenting relationships between two or more variables. They make use of whole numbers as well as proportions. However, for any single set of numerical cross-tabulations, percentages can be taken in three different ways: vertically, horizontally, or against the total number in the tables as a base. Each reveals a different aspect of the relationship between the two variables. Take, for example the following numerical cross-tabulation between the type of therapy prescribed in a family agency and the client's continuation in treatment. For the sake of simplicity, type of treatment is divided into two categories—family therapy and individual therapy. Client continuation is measured by whether clients returned after their intake interviews (see table 8.1).

	Family Therapy	Individual Therapy	Total
Return	30	100	130
Nonreturn	60	80	140
Total	90	180	270

TABLE 8.1

If the table were converted to vertical percentages, it would indicate the percentage of cases receiving each therapeutic prescription that returned or did not return for treatment. Such a table would treat the therapeutic recommendation as the *independent* or causal variable and the rate of client return as the *dependent* variable or the consequence (see table 8.2).

	Family Therapy	Individual Therapy
Return	33%	56%
Nonreturn	67%	44%
Total	100%	100%

TABLE 8.2

Moving from the presumed causal variable to the presumed consequence, this table shows that 33 percent of the cases that are to receive family therapy return for treatment compared with 56 percent of those that are to receive individual treatment. The latter then are 23 percent more likely to return than the former.

A table that used horizontally determined percentages would tell us the percentage in the return or nonreturn categories who received a therapeutic recommendation of family versus individual therapy. Rather than tell us about the impact of the recommendation on the rate of client return, that table would tell us the percentage of those who returned that are receiving family versus individual therapy. Such a table would more adequately *describe* the character of current treatment cases than would the previous, vertically percentaged table. Horizontally presented, the table would look like table 8.3.

	Family Therapy	Individual Therapy	Total
Return	23%	77%	100%
Nonreturn	43%	57%	100%

TABLE 8.3

Table 8.3 tells us that of the clients who returned for treatment, 23 percent were recommended for family therapy and 77 percent for individual therapy. Rather than shed light on the impact of the recommendation on the client's return as in the previous table, this table tells us something about the impact of the returning client on the type of therapy s/he is likely to receive.

A third way of percentaging is against the total number of cases as the numerical base. Such a table would describe the percentage of all cases which were processed at intake within each recommendation and return category (see table 8.4).

	Family Therapy	Individual Therapy	
Return	11%	37%	
Nonreturn	22%	30%	
			100% Total

TABLE 8.4

The table indicates that out of all the cases processed at intake, 11 percent received family therapy recommendations and returned, 37 percent received individual therapy recommendations and returned, 22 percent received family therapy recommendations and did not return, and 30 percent received individual therapy recommendations and did not return. This table describes a *typology* or multidimensional classification of different types of cases based on these two variables. From it, we see that the most typical case receives a recommendation of individual therapy and returns. Alternatively, the least typical case receives a family therapy recommendation and returns.

The reader is reminded that although each of the percentage tables reveals a different aspect of the relationship between treatment recommendation and client return, all were derived from the same set of whole numbers. Consequently, one must be careful to choose the type of percentaging which is most appropriate for the question the table is intended to answer.

Finally, using the original cross-tabluation of whole numbers, we can compute a simply yet highly versatile statistic, the *chi-square* (χ^2) to determine whether the relationship between the treatment recommendation received and the rate of client return is statistically significant. In other words, the chi-square can tell us whether the higher rate of nonreturn for those who received a family therapy recommendation is likely to be a chance phenomenon or is reflective of a statistically significant relationship between these two variables.

Briefly, the chi-square is based on a formula that contrasts the actual, observed frequencies in the various cells in the table with those one would expect if there were no relationship between the two variables that are cross-tabulated. If the computed value of the chi-square is sufficiently low, the actual findings are considered nonsignificant and as chance occurrences. If there are great differences between the expected and observed frequencies in each cell, this would be reflected in a high chi-square, which in turn would indicate a statistically significant relationship between the two variables in the table.

To calculate the chi-square for our table of whole numbers presented above, we must first calculate the expected numbers of cases receiving each treatment recommendation in each return category. To compute the expected number of clients who received a family therapy recommendation and returned, for example, one would use the following formula:

$$\frac{\text{Total Family Therapy}}{\text{Total Cases}} \times \text{Total Returns}$$

The numbers taken from the original cross-tabulation are substituted, and the expected number of cases receiving a family therapy recommendation and returning is found to be:

$$\frac{90}{270} \times 130 = 43.3$$

Following similar procedures, one can calculate the expected numbers for each cell of the original table. The following table indicates the observed and expected frequencies for each recommendation and return category. The expected frequencies appear in parentheses.

	Family Therapy	Individual Therapy
Return	30 (43.3)	100 (86.7)
Nonreturn	60 (46.7)	80 (93.3)

The final computation of the chi-square involves adding the sum total of the squared differences between all pairs of observed (O) and expected (E) frequencies, divided by the expected frequencies for each pair. This is expressed as a formula, using the summation sign ($\sum$):

$$\chi^2 = \sum \frac{(O-E)^2}{E}$$

Substituting the numerical values from our expected and observed findings for the letters in the formula, we get

$$\chi^2 = \frac{(30-43.3)^2}{43.3} + \frac{(100-86.7)^2}{86.7} + \frac{(60-46.7)^2}{46.7} + \frac{(80-93.3)^2}{93.3}$$
$$\chi^2 = 4.08 + 2.04 + 3.79 + 1.90$$
$$\chi^2 = 11.81$$

With a table like this (that is a 2×2 table), a chi-square with any value of 3.84 or better is taken to indicate that the relationship between the variables in the table *is* statistically significant.* Since the value of the chi-square in our table exceeds 3.84, we would conclude that the relationship observed between the type of treatment recommendation received and the rate of client return is not a product of chance variation. The next task would be to discover why this relationship exists.

---

*For tables with expected frequencies below 5 in any cells, additional adjustments have to be made in the computation. However, with a table of those proportions, expected frequencies greater than 5, and a chi-square value over 3.34, the findings in the table could occur by chance alone less than 5 times in 100. According to research conventions, this probability level is considered statistically significant. Discussions of adjustments for small numbers of cases and various levels of statistical significance are contained within standard text books on statistical methods.

3. Controlling for Intervening Variables

The cross-tabulations presented above seem to reveal a relationship between the type of treatment recommendation that a client receives and whether the client is likely to return to the agency for this treatment. However, it would be premature to assert on the basis of this table alone that there is a cause-effect relationship between the treatment recommendation and the client's return. Thus, the relationship between recommendation and return may be the consequence of a third variable that is accidentally associated with both treatment recommendation and return. If that were the case, the original relationship would be called a *spurious relationship* in that it gives a false impression of causality. To establish that a relationship is *causal* or *spurious*, researchers "control" for the possibly *intervening* effects of *explanatory* variables which are theoretically linked to both variables in the original relationship and spurious variables which are only accidentally linked to both variables. Only through such *multivariate analysis* can one tease out cause-effect relationships.

In the example above, it may turn out that clients who received a recommendation of family therapy may have been seen by less skillful workers. As a consequence, their not returning might be a response to the lack of skill of the social worker they saw rather than a response to the type of therapy recommended. In this instance, the three variables (that is, recommendation, return and worker skill) are not theoretically linked. Therefore, the original relationship between recommendation and return would be spurious.

Alternatively, it may turn out that the reason clients who received a family therapy recommendation were less likely to return was that their spouses were more likely to oppose this recommendation than the spouses of clients who received an individual therapy recommendation. Here, the three variables are logically linked. To see if this explanation is correct, however, the theoretical relationship between the three variables should be empirically tested.

Controlling for or "holding constant" the spouse's attitude toward treatment would require the construction of two additional tables, one looking at the relationship between recommendation and return when spouses oppose treatment and one looking at the relationship between recommendation and return when spouses are supportive of treatment. Should the relationship between recommendation and return persist in each of these tables, that would indicate that the original relationship between recommendation and return was not explained by the spouse's opposition (see table 8.5).

| | Spouse Opposes | | Spouse Supports | |
	Family Therapy	Individual Therapy	Family Therapy	Individual Therapy
Return	30%	52%	35%	58%
Nonreturn	70%	48%	65%	42%

TABLE 8.5

The tables indicate that irrespective of the spouse's attitude toward treatment, clients who receive a family therapy recommendation are still less likely to return. Thus, we see that for those clients whose husbands oppose treatment, there is a 22 percent difference between the return rates for those who received one recommendation versus the other. Likewise, in families in which the spouse is supportive, a 23 percent difference exists. Under these circumstances, the spouse's opposition or support does not explain why family therapy clients are less likely to return.

If, on the other hand, we controlled for spouse's opposition and our cross-tabulations looked like table 8.6, they would indicate that when spouse's attitude is held constant the differences in return rates by type of recommendation disappear. Thus, when the spouse opposes, there is only a 1 percent difference between family and individual recommendation in the return rate. When the spouse is supportive a 2 percent difference exists and that favors those in family therapy. By comparing the findings between tables and within a recommendation type, it is clear that for either recom-

	Spouse Opposes		Spouse Supports	
	Family Therapy	*Individual Therapy*	*Family Therapy*	*Individual Therapy*
Return	31%	32%	70%	68%
Nonreturn	69%	68%	30%	32%

TABLE 8.6

mendation spouse's support contributes a good deal to whether the client will return. These findings would lead us to conclude that the original negative relationship between a family therapy recommendation and return was explained by the fact that spouses were more likely to oppose a family therapy recommendation and that in turn led to a lower rate of treatment compliance. Here again a chi-square can be computed for each table to determine whether patterns within are likely to be products of chance variations alone.

In general, it is extremely important to control for as many possible intervening variables as one can to determine the true explanation for a finding or alternatively to discover whether the finding is spurious. Without such controls, assertions about causality are premature.

HYPOTHETICAL ILLUSTRATION

A clinical administrator in a woman's crisis center has introduced a feminist therapy counseling program in her agency. The program offers women individual counseling as well as mutual support groups. In the course of the first year, the program has served 120 women from all segments of the community. Recently, however, program critics have contended that the services it offers are primarily geared toward middle-class women. She decides to collect and analyze data relevant to this issue and to interpret the findings to her staff. Should the data reveal any class bias, she would want to take measures to correct these.

1. Collecting the Data and Computing a Frequency Distribution

To collect relevant data, the administrator reviews client termination statistics available in the agency's records. Her intention is to see whether lower-class women have significantly fewer agency contacts than do women of the middle class.

From the agency's records, the administrator is able to calculate a grouped frequency distribution based on the clients' reports of their family income. Using the median income as her dividing point, she divides the client population into those who are above and those who are below the median.

Next, she computes a frequency distribution based on the number of times individual clients have come to the agency within the past year. Again, using the median as a dividing point, she identifies clients who are above and those who are below the median in attendance.

2. Computing Cross-Tabulations and the Chi-Square

Next she cross-tabulates client income and client attendance. Indeed, her findings reveal that clients from lower income families attend the center much less frequently than clients from more middle income families. A computation of the chi-square for this table reveals that the inverse relationship between class and attendance is statistically significant.

3. Controlling for Intervening Variables

To determine whether this relationship holds under various conditions or can be explained by variables that she has access to, she extracts whatever quantifiable information is available from the case records and which might serve to explain this unfortunate finding. One control variable that she is able to cull from the case records refers to the clients' level of education. Again, on this variable she plots a frequency distribution, and divides the population at the median into those with relatively high and those with relatively low educational attainments. By controlling for educational level, in a multivariate analysis she discovers that among highly educated women, there is no longer a relationship between income and attendance. For women with low levels of education, however, income is still significantly related to attendance.

These findings are then brought to staff for discussion. Various possible explanations are offered ranging from the need for programming to serve low income, low education clientele to providing babysitting for these women so that they can more regularly attend counseling and support group sessions.

EXERCISE

Select a program that can provide you with descriptive data on clients' incomes, types of problems presented, and whether or not clients were accepted for service. Compute the frequency distributions for the clients' incomes and the mean, median, and modal income of the total client population. Compute the percentage of each client income group accepted or rejected. Compute a chi-square to determine whether there is a statistically significant relationship between the two. Finally construct a table controlling for problem type. Interpret the findings.

SELECTED BIBLIOGRAPHY

Amos, Jimmy R., Foster L. Brown, and Oscar G. Mink, *Statistical Concepts: A Basic Program* (New York: Harper and Row, 1965), pp. 125.

Goldstein, Harris K., *Research Standards and Methods for Social Workers* (New Orleans: Hauser Press, 1963). pp. 179–295.

Hirschi, Travis and Hanan C. Selvin, *Delinquency Research* (New York: Free Press, 1967), pp. 35–142.

Huff, Darrell, *How to Lie with Statistics* (New York: Norton, 1954), pp. 142.

Wallis, W. Allen and Harry Roberts, *The Nature of Statistics* (New York: Free Press, 1965), pp. 89–122 and pp. 177–207.

Walizer, Michael H. and Paul L. Wiener, *Research Methods and Analysis* (New York: Harper and Row, 1978), pp. 83–121.

Weiss, Robert S., *Statistics in Social Research* (New York: Wiley, 1968), pp. 244–75.

Part Three
TREATMENT EVALUATION

Treatment evaluation is the third and final phase of clinical social work practice. It is the process by which treatment effectiveness and efficiency are assessed. In other words, treatment evaluation is necessary to determine whether treatment goals have been attained, and at what cost. Moreover, treatment evaluation provides information that enables the clinical social worker to decide whether to continue or terminate treatment. Finally, treatment evaluation provides information about the efficacy of specific treatment strategies.

Treatment evaluation is one of the two basic foci of evaluation in social agencies. One focus, *program evaluation*, concentrates on the agency itself and attempts to evaluate the effectiveness and efficiency of whole programs within the agency. *Treatment evaluation*, on the other hand, focusses on evaluating the effectiveness and efficiency of a single social worker with a single client, family or group. Program evaluation and treatment evaluation coincide, however, when the results of the work of more than one social worker and/or the treatment outcomes with more than one client unit are aggregated and analyzed. *Such aggregation of findings is only appropriate when treatment objectives and treatment strategies are the same for each social worker and client unit.*

Within each level of evaluation a further distinction can be made between formative and summative evaluation. *Formative evaluation* involves the feedback of results within a program or for a client while the program or client treatment is still under way. This information does not permit generalization of findings beyond that particular program or client unit. It does, however, permit program administrators or clinical social workers to make program or treatment changes as the program or the treatment develops.

Alternatively, *summative evaluation* provides information feedback after a program or treatment cycle has been completed. And, while it permits generalization of findings beyond a particular program or client unit, what is learned from it must wait for a new program or client unit to be applied to practice. Thus, summative evaluation provides more certainty about the causal links between intervention and outcome, but less immediate applicability to practice.

In this section of the book, we emphasize formative evaluation of individual treatment units. This evaluation approach can be used by individual clinicians for assessing their own effectiveness with individual clients or with aggregates of their clients or client groups. Elsewhere, we have emphasized formative program evaluation (see, for example, Tripodi, Fellin, and Epstein 1978; Epstein and Tripodi 1977).

Treatment evaluation can be seen as a continuation of treatment monitoring as well. By providing valid and reliable information about treatment outcomes, the connections between treatment interventions and their impact can be clarified. Hence, treatment evaluation can be located on a continuum of research activities between treatment monitoring and program evaluation.

TASKS

Treatment evaluation requires that the clinical social worker accomplish a number of practice-related tasks and make a number of decisions. The tasks are as follows:

1. First, treatment strategies and treatment objectives must be specified. Naturally, if the intended treatment has not been faithfully implemented, there is little point in evaluating what has not taken place. If, on the other hand, a monitoring of actual treatment indicates that the intended form of intervention has been implemented, then treatment evaluation is appropriate. If, however, some other form of treatment has occurred, treatment evaluation

makes sense *only* if the actual treatment can be systematically described. Thus, despite our heuristic distinction between treatment monitoring and treatment evaluation, the two are inextricably linked in practice. Moreover, in specifying treatment objectives, it is helpful for the purposes of evaluation to indicate a time frame within which treatment objectives are to be achieved. This will ease the task of evaluation considerably by indicating when systematic evaluation should take place.

2. Next, treatment objectives are operationally defined, that is, translated into measureable terms. This procedure may be begun in the monitoring phase for the purpose of collecting information about client progress. However, not all variables will demonstrate change during treatment, especially in the early stages. As a result, treatment evaluation frequently takes place after treatment has been terminated. Finally, some treatment evaluation designs require that "outcome measures" be taken *before* treatment has begun and *after* it has been terminated. Here again treatment monitoring and evaluation are part of the same process.

3. Once treatment objectives are operationally defined, evaluation objectives should be determined. Thus, the purpose of the evaluation should be specified and the information necessary to achieve this purpose should be delineated. Evaluation objectives may be broadly or narrowly focused. A comprehensive evaluation would focus broadly on the extent to which numerous treatment objectives have been achieved, the relationships between treatment intervention and these objectives, the relationships among the objectives, and the efficiency of the treatment as well. Alternatively, evaluation may focus more narrowly on the achievement of a particular, highly specific treatment objective.

Another component of evaluation objectives is the level of knowledge to be achieved. As we indicated in chapter 5, research knowledge exists on four levels: hypothetical; descriptive; correlational; and cause–effect. In the context of treatment evaluation objectives, hypothetical knowledge would involve generation of hypotheses about the relationships between specific treatment interventions and outcomes. This is the least certain level of knowledge. Descriptive knowledge simply describes treatment outcomes without asserting a connection between the treatment interventions and these outcomes. Correlational knowledge demonstrates a relationship between intervention and outcome, but does not firmly establish that one causes the other. Finally, cause–effect knowledge establishes the causal connection between intervention and client outcome. In doing so, it rules out other possible explanations of client improvement. As a result, it is the most certain form of knowledge.

4 The level of knowledge desired will determine the kind of evaluation design and methodology which is most appropriate. The next task, then, is to select an evaluation design and methodology which is likely to produce the level of knowledge required. The more certainty desired, the more comprehensive and costly the evaluation is likely to be. Moreover, cause–effect knowledge requires rigorous experimental designs which frequently have serious ethical limitations. Formative treatment evaluation designs seek to maximize the level of knowledge produced without broaching these ethical limits.

5. Once the design and methodology have been chosen, the evaluation is implemented. This involves collecting and processing information from such devices as forms, observational instruments, questionnaires, and the like. This information may be collected prior to and throughout the treatment process or only after treatment has been completed. The evaluation design will determine when the information is to be collected.

6. Next, the information must be analyzed in relation to the evaluation and treatment objectives. Based on this analysis, the clinician can decide whether there is evidence indicating that the treatment objectives have been fully, partially or minimally attained. In some cases, in fact, the client's condition may have deteriorated.

7. Finally, treatment must be terminated, continued, or intensified. If the treatment goals are achieved, treatment may be ter-

minated, with a follow-up contact with the client after a few months to determine whether treatment gains have been maintained. If treatment goals have been partially attained, treatment may be continued, intensified or combined with other treatment approaches in a new cycle of treatment. If there has been no improvement, or if the client seems to have deteriorated, the use of an alternative treatment strategy, a different clinician, a referral to another agency, or a clinical consultation may be considered.

TREATMENT EVALUATION DECISIONS

Clinical social workers need to make a number of important decisions in evaluating the efficacy of their treatment. Those decisions are implied within each of the foregoing tasks, but they can be specified by indicating some of the questions which the clinical social worker should ask him/herself during this final phase of practice. Moreover, since clinical practice is a dynamic process, the questions are related to questions raised during diagnostic assessment, treatment formulation, and treatment monitoring. Some of these questions are as follows:

1. Are treatment objectives achieved? If so, to what extent? If not, why not? Were the objectives realistic for the client?
2. Was the treatment appropriate for the client? Should the intensity of the treatment be modified? Should the clinician employ a different strategy?
3. Should the evaluation be reinstituted at some point in the future? Were the evaluation methodology and design appropriate for measuring treatment objectives?
4. If treatment objectives have been reached, is there evidence to indicate that the client will be able to maintain these gains without the clinician's continued involvement and intervention?
5. If treatment objectives have not been reached, should a consultation be sought? Should the client be referred to another social worker or to another agency?
6. Have appropriate measures been taken for client termination, referral or continuation? Is the client agreeable to such action?

7. Has any knowledge been gained with this client that might be useful in working with other clients?

RESEARCH CONCEPTS AND TECHNIQUES

As we implied earlier, for the purposes of treatment evaluation, all of the data-gathering devices which we have described in previous chapters can be used. Thus, treatment evaluation data can come from standardized interviews, observation schedules, monitoring forms, and the like. Moreover, the same principles and techniques of data analysis described in the preceding chapter are used in analyzing evluation data.

In this section, we present some additional data-gathering and analyzing procedures. These are applied to evaluating the effectiveness of clinical intervention. We believe that the research concepts and techniques which we have selected, can be easily employed by clinical social workers of different theoretical persuasions and with limited research background.

In chapter 9, we discuss procedures for conducting follow-up surveys of client progress. These can be accomplished through face-to-face or telephone interviews or by self-administered client questionnaires. In this context, concepts and techniques of survey sampling are discussed.

Chapter 10 is devoted to the construction of rating scales that can be used in estimating the achievement of treatment objectives. Here, we distinguish between scales that are used for client self-rating or for the rating of clients by others. Although we refer to existing procedures such as "goal-attainment scaling," our emphasis is on the presentation of principles that the clinician can use to develop his/her own rating devices for specific clinical situations.

Interrupted time-series designs are discussed in chapter 11. These designs are useful in both treatment and program evaluation. In discussion of these designs, we indicate criteria for determining the extent to which the knowledge they generate is correlational or cause-effect.

Finally, chapter 12 describes three designs which originated in behavior modification, but which can be employed to measure effectiveness of other intervention strategies as well. The advantages and limitations of these designs for evaluating clinical practices are described.

SELECTED BIBLIOGRAPHY

Coursey, Robert D., ed., *Program Evaluation for Mental Health* (New York: Grune and Stratton, 1977), pp. 1–25.

Compton, Beulah Roberts and Burt Galoway, *Social Work Processes* (Homewood, Ill.: Dorsey Press, 1975), pp. 382–446.

Epstein, Irwin and Tony Tripodi, *Research Techniques for Program Planning, Monitoring, and Evaluation* (New York: Columbia University Press, 1977), pp. 111–17.

Gottman, John M. and Sandra R. Leiblum, *How To Do Psychotherapy and How To Evaluate It* (New York: Holt, Rinehart and Winston, 1974), pp. 129–58.

Pincus, Allen and Anne Minahan, *Social Work Practice* (Itasca, Ill.: F. E. Peacock, 1973), pp. 272–88.

Tripodi, Tony, *Uses and Abuses of Social Research in Social Work* (New York: Columbia University Press, 1974), pp. 122–31.

Tripodi, Tony, Phillip Fellin, and Irwin Epstein, *Differential Social Program Evaluation* (Itasca, Ill.: F. E. Peacock, 1978), pp. 1–21 and 105–42.

Tripodi, Tony, Phillip Fellin, Irwin Epstein, and Roger Lind, *Social Workers at Work* (2d ed.; Itasca, Ill.: F. E. Peacock, 1977), pp. 64–71.

Weber, Ruth E. and Norman A. Polansky, "Evaluation" in Norman A. Polansky, ed., *Social Work Research* (2d ed.; Chicago: University of Chicago Press, 1975), pp. 182–201.

9

THE USE OF SAMPLE SURVEYS IN FOLLOW-UP EVALUATIONS

"Follow-up" evaluations are studies which take place *after* treatment has been completed and the client's relationship with the agency has been terminated. Data collection may involve face-to-face interviews, self-administered client questionnaires, or telephone interviews. Frequently, these data gathering efforts take place weeks or months after treatment has been terminated so that judgments can be made about whether treatment gains have persisted over time or whether the client's condition has deteriorated without continued treatment.

Often, however, there are not sufficient resources to survey every client who has received treatment from an individual social worker or from a staff of social workers. In instances such as these, sample surveys are used. *Sample surveys* are research devices for making relatively safe generalizations about a larger *target population* from findings within a smaller *sample* taken from the target population. The greater the similarity between the sample and the target population, the safer the generalizations that can be made. When sample and target populations are demonstrated to be highly comparable, we refer to the sample as *representative*.

Sample surveys are probably the most often used data-gathering strategy employed by social researchers. Their uses range from public opinion polls and market research to mental health surveys. In the context of clinical social work, they can serve to gather information from a client sample about satisfaction with services received, self-concepts, attitudes, behaviors, and so on. They may be used by clinicians themselves to evaluate samples of their own cases, by supervisors to evaluate sample client outcomes within a treatment unit, or by administrators to evaluate an entire program by sampling service recipients.

Whatever the target population, sampling techniques are designed either to increase the chances of drawing a representative sample or to decrease the cost of data gathering. Unfortunately, however, these two objectives are generally in conflict. The larger the sample, the greater the likelihood of representativeness, but the greater the cost of data collection as well. This contradiction is a continuing dilemma for the researcher who does not have the resources to study an entire target population. Here a sampling strategy must be devised that both maximizes the chances of representativeness and remains within the resource limitations of the study. Even after the sample has been drawn, however, statistical techniques must be used to determine whether the sampling strategy has in fact produced a representative sample.

An additional problem in follow-up surveys is that they do not provide direct evidence of the causal link between treatment interventions and client outcomes. This is because they generally involve measures that are only taken *after* treatment has been completed. By precluding before/after comparisons they do not provide direct evidence of client change. Moreover, follow-up surveys generally focus only on individuals who have received treatment. By not collecting evidence from a *control group* of comparable individuals who did not receive treatment, they cannot establish with absolute certainty that it was in fact the treatment that produced positive client outcomes.

Nevertheless, follow-up surveys of client samples represent an efficient formative approach for assessing client conditions after treatment has been terminated and for assessing client satisfaction with the treatment they have received. And, while this approach sacrifices certainty of knowledge about the causal connections between treatment and client outcome, it is relatively inexpensive to implement, it does not intrude data collection devices and procedures into the treatment process, and it does not involve denial of treatment which is necessary for creating a control group.

SAMPLE SURVEYS AND CLINICAL SOCIAL WORK PRACTICE

Sampling principles and techniques are potentially useful in all phases of clinical social work practice. In diagnosis and treatment planning, for example, the social worker may need to make diagnostic inferences about a child's behavior based on a number of observations of the child at home, at school and in play situations with other children. Only by properly sampling these behaviors and giving attention to how representative they are can appropriate diagnostic inferences be made.

Likewise, in treatment monitoring, representative samples of groups of clients may be drawn to determine the kinds of services they are receiving, the frequency of service and the quality of service. Such a monitoring study involves principles and techniques of sampling, aggregation and data analysis.

Finally, sampling techniques and principles are useful in many evaluation designs. Thus, they are as likely to be used in summative evaluations as in formative evaluations. In summative evaluation designs, for example, they may be used in assigning experimental subjects to treatment and to control groups. In formative evaluations, the same principles and techniques may be used to select samples of service recipients to study. As a consequence, sampling principles and techniques constitute some of the most useful tools in the clinical researcher's repertoire.

In this chapter, we will focus on principles and techniques of sample survey methodology as they apply to follow-up evaluations.

In it, we shall stress the use of time-saving procedures such as systematic sampling and telephone interviewing. Since sample surveys frequently involve the use of self-administered questionnaires, interviews or forms, we recommend that the reader review our previous chapters on these topics (chapters 2 and 7).

PRINCIPLES FOR CONDUCTING FOLLOW-UP SAMPLE SURVEYS

1. Defining the Purpose of the Survey

Broadly speaking, the purpose of a follow-up evaluation is to acquire information about client outcomes that is not already available through existing monitoring devices. More specifically, such a study can reflect on the quality and effectiveness of treatment and the soundness of termination and/or referral decisions. Finally, it is an important source of information about client satisfaction with agency services.

Before constructing any data collecting instruments, however, it is necessary to determine the specific information regarding client progress and satisfaction that is desired. Since client progress may mean different things in different cases, questions directed to more than one client will have to be sufficiently general and abstract so that aggregation and comparison of client data is possible. Questions about whether the client has maintained the benefits gained during treatment are also useful. Client progress may be indicated as well by questions which concern the presence or absence of negative side-effects associated with treatment. Thus, for example, a client who has completed a smoking reduction program may have successfully stopped smoking but at the same time gained twenty unneeded pounds in the process.

Measures of client satisfaction are another important source of information. Although they may or may not be associated with treatment success, they can be good predictors of whether the client would seek the agency's help with other problems which might arise in his or her life. In addition, client satisfaction is likely to lead to the client's recommendation that relatives or friends with similar problems contact the agency. These measures need not be confined to questions about whether the client liked the social worker, but should be directed to satisfaction with the type of treatment received, perceptions of the social worker's competence and concern for the client, whether appointment times were convenient, questions about the cost of service, whether the number of visits seemed adequate, and so on. Overall, the information collected should inform the worker's and/or agency's future treatment and policy decisions and actions.

2. Designating the Target Population and the Sampling Unit

After specifying the purpose of the follow-up study, the social worker should specify the characteristics of the client population to be surveyed. The basis for determining the *target population* can vary. Thus, one may want to survey all those clients who have been terminated during a given *time period*, say the last six months. Another basis for determining the target population is *problem*. So, for example, one may wish to survey all clients who were treated for a given type of problem, such as depression or anorexia. The target population may be defined in terms of the kind or kinds of *treatment* received. For instance, a follow-up study may compare the satisfaction of clients who received short term versus long term treatment, behavior modification versus analytically oriented treatment, and so on. Target populations can be defined as well by focusing on *characteristics of the clients* themselves. Here, factors such as age, race, income, education and the like may be the determining features of the target population.

Whatever the basis of the target population, one must consider whether sufficient resources are available to study the whole group about which one would like to make generalizations. If scarcity of time and money prevent study of the entire target population, then some type of sampling strategy is required. This involves specifying the basic *sampling units* from which to choose. The type of target population determines the sampling unit. Thus, if the target population is all families that received family therapy, the sampling unit is each individual family that falls in this treatment category.

To increase the chances that the sample drawn will be unbiased and representative, each sampling unit in the target population should have an equal probability of being selected. Not all sampling strategies make this possible, however.

3. Choosing a Sampling Strategy

There are basically two kinds of sampling strategies—nonprobability and probability sampling. In *nonprobability sampling*, there is no way of determining the probability that any particular sampling unit will actually be included in the sample population. Nonprobability techniques are cheap and quick. They can be used for generating hypotheses, pretesting research instruments, and getting rough ideas about a given population. They are likely, however, to produce biased and nonrepresentative samples.

Three types of nonprobability sampling strategies are accidental sampling, quota sampling, and purposive sampling. *Accidental sampling* involves choosing the most readily accessible set of sampling units available, without regard to whether the sampling units are representative of the target population. Thus, a follow-up study of the last fifty clients served in a program that has been in operation for years may give a very biased picture of the hundreds of clients served by this program. On the one hand, it may give a falsely positive evaluation if the program has improved over the years, or a falsely negative evaluation if the program has declined in quality. In addition, it would be inadequate for assessing whether treatment gains persist after treatment because the clients surveyed will have only recently terminated agency contact. For these and other reasons, the findings of a study based on such a sample could not be safely generalized to the target population served by the agency since the program's inception.

The second type of nonprobability sampling is *quota sampling*. It is a more refined form of accidental sampling and is frequently used in less scientific public opinion polls. In quota sampling, the target population is classified by certain pertinent characteristics such as race, ethnicity, or age. Quotas are set, frequently based on the proportion of each group in the target population. Thus, if clients who are characterized as having "character disorders" constitute 10 percent of the target population served by the agency, a quota sample of 50 clients should contain 5 clients who have received this diagnosis. These 5 are selected on an accidental basis. Once this quota is achieved, no additional clients with this diagnostic label are included in the sample. This sampling strategy produces a sample population that resembles the target population in the properties specified, in this case diagnostic categories. However, since the selection of respondents to fill the quotas is accidental, the result is still likely to be biased and unrepresentative. Thus, all clients within each diagnostic category do not have an equal chance of being selected. Moreover, in quota sampling those who refuse to participate in the study are simply ignored. This is why public opinion polls are frequently wrong.

Purposive sampling is a third type of nonprobability sampling. It involves hand selecting cases for inclusion in a study on the basis of some notion of what is typical or what is unique about the cases. Like accidental and quota sampling, it is cheap and quick. It is also highly unreliable, since it is frequently based on erroneous stereotypes. In a follow-up study, such a strategy is likely to lead to the hand selection of those cases which are most successful. While such a study might provide some hypotheses about the conditions which are likely to lead to treatment success, it would provide a biased and unrepresentative picture of the target population of clients who have received treatment.

In contrast to nonprobability sampling, *probability sampling* makes it possible to calculate the probability that any one sampling unit in the total target population will be selected for the sample. Moreover, probability sampling makes it possible to calculate the margin of error that is likely to occur under different sampling conditions and the sample size that is necessary to reduce error to a tolerable minimum. In other words, probability sampling enables the researcher to estimate the degree to which generalizations to the target population can be made safely from findings within the sample population. Though they cannot guarantee representativeness, probability sampling techniques greatly increase the likelihood of this outcome.

The most common type of probability sampling strategy is the *simple random sample*. With this strategy, every sampling unit within the target population has an equal probability of being included in the sample population. To draw a simple random sample, each unit within the target population is assigned a number. Then, using a table of random numbers available in any statistics book, or using numbers in a hat, the researcher selects individual units randomly until a sample of the appropriate size is selected. This technique requires no previous knowledge or categorization of the target population. Nevertheless it is more likely to produce a representative sample on *every* characteristic of the target population than *any* of the non-probability sampling strategies. Even simple random sampling, however, does not insure representativeness.

Another form of probability sampling is *systematic sampling*. This technique is particularly useful in sampling case records that are filed either alphabetically or by identification numbers. To do systematic sampling, one must first establish the *sampling ratio*, that is, the proportion of the total target population that will be included in the sample population. If the sampling ratio were one-fourth, that would mean that one out of every four client units in the target population would be selected for study. Taking a random starting point, the researcher would then select every fourth case until s/he had completed one full cycle of all case records. With populations organized alphabetically, systematic sampling can produce samples as representative as simple random samples with far less difficulty in the mechanism of selection (Babbie 1973). Here again, however, the technique does not guarantee representativeness.

A more refined kind of probability sampling is *stratified random sampling*. In this strategy, the target population is first described according to certain pertinent properties—for example, short-term versus long-term treatment cases. Then a random sample is selected from within each treatment grouping. The numbers chosen for each may correspond to the proportion of this treatment group in the total target population. We call this *proportionate stratified random sampling*. This strategy would yield a highly precise picture of the total target population. When emphasis is placed on making comparisons between different types of cases within the total target population, *disproportionate stratified random sampling* may be employed. Thus, if only 10 percent of the clients in the target population are long-term cases, and the study is designed to make comparisons between long- and short-term treatment, a disproportionate sampling strategy will be used to generate subsamples of equal size of these two treatment groups. In such a sampling strategy, the members of the different treatment categories have different probabilities of being included in the sample, but the probabilities within each treatment group are known. This is not the case with quota sampling.

Depending on the nature of the study, any of the foregoing sampling strategies may be used on a one-time, multiple, or sequential basis. Overall, it is clear that the advantages of probability sampling far outweigh the disadvantages. Consequently, in follow-up surveys probability sampling is recommended. When in doubt, however, about what form of probability sampling should be used, a simple random sample should be the strategy of choice.

4. Selecting a Sample Size

The decision about the size of the sample population is complex. Some aspects of this decision are highly technical and may require the consultation of a researcher. This is particularly true when one wants a precise estimate of the possibility of making an erroneous generalization from a sample population of a given size to a target population.*

* For the formula for calculating the size of the sample required on the basis of size of target population and tolerable margin for error, see Walker and Lev (1953:70).

Other aspects of this decision are more practical. These involve questions of resources. How much time and money are available and how many interviews do they make possible in a day? If a questionnaire is mailed to respondents, initial mailing and return mailing costs must be calculated. More often than not, these practical considerations will determine the sample size.

Recognizing the inevitability of the above, we suggest two rough rules of thumb. First, do not choose samples smaller than 50 for a follow-up survey. Second, if there are categories of sampling units that are particularly relevant to the study, employ a strategy that will generate at least 25 units of each of these categories in the sample population. So, in a study of treatment outcomes with a target population of 100 cases, sample at least 50 cases. If the study focuses on the impact of treatment on middle-class versus working-class clients, be sure that the sampling strategy provides at least 25 cases from each socioeconomic stratum. This requires taking into account the probability that a given proportion of clients selected for inclusion in the study will refuse to participate.

5. Listing Target Population and Selecting the Sample

Once a sampling strategy has been chosen, a complete list of the target population should be compiled. For systematic sampling, sampling units should be listed in alphabetical order or any other order that does not involve an implicit pattern that might bias the sample. In simple random sampling, the ordering of units is of no significance since each individual unit will still have an equal probability of being selected. For stratified random sampling, a separate but complete list should be compiled for each group which is being differentiated in the target population. Thus, if the sample population is going to be stratified by diagnostic category, then separate lists should be compiled for each. The ordering within each of these lists will be of no significance since random selection will take place within each diagnostic category.

After compiling the list of the target population, the sample can be selected. In systematic sampling, this involves choosing a sampling ratio, taking a random starting point and selecting cases consistent with the sampling ratio.

In simple random sampling, each unit in the listing of the target population is given a separate identification number. Then using a table of random numbers or numbers in a hat, a sample of desired magnitude is randomly selected. For stratified random sampling, a comparable set of procedures would be employed for each stratum of the target population until the desired subsamples were drawn.

6. Checking the Representativeness of the Sample

Since probability sampling promotes but does not insure representativeness, it is important that a sample population be checked to see whether it is representative of the target population on dimensions that are relevant to the study. This process requires some knowledge of the characteristics of both the sample and the target populations.

To check for representativeness one begins with percentage comparisons between the sample and target populations on those dimensions that are relevant to the study and about which there is complete information for both populations. For example, a target population of 1,000 clients may contain 40 percent males and 60 percent females. A perfect, representative sample of 100 clients would contain 40 males and 60 females. If the sample population contained 25 males and 75 females, one would question the representativeness of the sample. In this case, males would be underrepresented and females overrepresented. Consequently, if it were found that gender was differentially associated with treatment outcome, adjustments would have to be made in the inferences drawn from such a sample population. Moreover, if a self-administered mailed questionnaire were used, percentage differences between respondents and nonrespondents should be compared. Here again, such comparisons tell us whether inferences based on respondent questionnaires are likely to be biased.

A second, more refined technique for assessing representativeness of a sample involves the use of the chi-square statistic introduced in chapter 8. This simple yet versatile statistic has, among its many uses, the capacity to determine whether data distributions in the sample population are sufficiently like those in the target population to warrant the assumption of representativeness. Similarly, with self-administered questionnaires, it can be used to determine whether respondents are significantly different from nonrespondent populations. In the context of sampling, a chi-square which indicates a statistically significant difference between target and sample populations, or between respondent and nonrespondent populations, means that the assumption of complete representativeness must be rejected.

To assess representativeness, chi-square is based on a formula that contrasts the actual observed frequencies in the sample population with those one would expect to find in a perfect representative sample. Likewise, it can be used to statistically compare actual and expected frequencies in respondent and nonrespondent populations. If the computed value of the chi-square is sufficiently low, a high degree of similarity between sample and target populations, or between respondent and nonrespondent populations is indicated. This means that the sample population is representative on the dimensions tested and that relatively safe generalizations can be made from the findings in the study.

Let us take an example. Suppose we were comparing the gender distribution of the target population of agency clients referred to above with a 10 percent simple random sample population of 45 males and 55 females. Given the distribution in the target population, the expected frequencies for a perfect representative sample would be 40 males and 60 females. In tabular form, the actual and expected (in parentheses) frequencies would look like this:

	Males	Females
Observed and expected frequencies	45 (40)	55 (60)

Using the formula cited in chapter 7:

$$\chi^2 = \sum \frac{(O-E)^2}{E},$$

and substituting the numerical values from our expected and observed populations for the letters in the formula, we get:

$$\chi^2 = \frac{(45-40)^2}{40} + \frac{(55-60)^2}{60}$$

$$\chi^2 = \frac{25}{40} + \frac{25}{60}$$

$$\chi^2 = 1.04$$

With a table of these proportions, a chi-square with any value less than 3.84 is generally taken to indicate that the sample population is not significantly different from the target population.* Since the value of the chi-square in our example is only 1.04, we can assume that at least insofar as gender is concerned, our sample population is representative. For sampling distributions with more than two categories, chi-square is computed in exactly the same manner. However, for the samples to be representative, a distribution with three categories should yield a chi-square value below 5.99; with four categories below 7.82; with five categories below 9.49; with six categories below 12.59; with seven categories below 14.07; and so on (Blalock 1960:452).

7. Choosing a Method of Data Collection

There are three primary methods of data collection that can be employed in follow-up surveys: face-to-face interviews, telephone interviews, and mailed self-administered questionnaires. The cheapest and least time-consuming is the mailed questionnaire. The problem with mailed questionnaires, however, is that they tend to produce low response rates. And, those who do respond may have views that are more extreme (either positive or negative) than those who are not motivated to respond. As a result, unless response

---

* With a table of these proportions, chi-square values that are 3.84 or greater are likely to occur by chance only 5 times in 100. According to research conventions, this probability level is considered to be statistically significant.

rates are quite high (over 65 percent) they are likely to be biased in the picture they present.

The face-to-face interview, on the other hand, is likely to yield the most complete, accurate, and unbiased information. It is, however, a very costly and time-consuming method of data collection.

As a compromise between the two when clients can be reached by phone, telephone interviews are suggested for follow-up evaluation surveys. They yield a higher response rate than mailed questionnaires (Dillman 1978), but are not nearly as costly or as time-consuming as face-to-face interviews. Moreover, telephone interviews do not require that respondents be literate (as with questionnaires) nor do they require client and interviewer to meet face-to-face. The latter can be a serious problem when clients have moved since they were in treatment or when agency clients are, in general, geographically dispersed.

Telephone surveys are limited in that they cannot use questions that involve visual displays or complex sets of instructions. In addition, questions which involve rank-ordering of alternatives should be avoided (Dillman 1978). Despite these limitations, telephone interviewing can be an efficient and effective device for collecting information about client progress and satisfaction with agency services. Finally, telephone contacts may be used in conjunction with other primary sources of data collection. Thus, telephone interviewing may be used as a substitute for face-to-face interviewing when a former client is inaccessible. Moreover, when self-administered questionnaires are the primary data-collection instruments, telephone contacts may be used as reminders to those who have not completed their questionnaires, or as sources of information about nonrespondents.

8. Constructing Telephone Interview Schedules

In constructing telephone interview schedules, one should employ the basic principles used in constructing standardized interviews and questionnaires discussed in chapter 2. The interview schedule should begin with an introduction which indicates how much time will be required, why the information is desired, and what will be done with it. Those contacted should be advised that they have a right to participate or not, that the results are confidential, and that the information will not be used to negatively effect the respondent's or their social worker's status in the agency in any way. The interviewer should solicit the interviewee's cooperation on the basis of the agency's interest in his/her progress and opinions regarding the services received, and that this information might be used to make changes in the existing structure and procedures of the agency. In this way, the potential respondent views participation as being in his/her self-interest or in the interest of future clients similar to him/herself.

Interview questions themselves, should be relatively short and direct. For questions that are somewhat complicated, some redundancy should be built in through summarizing statements. Overall, telephone interviews should not last longer than 15 minutes. Time and opportunity should be left at the end of the interview for the respondent to indicate whether s/he requires renewed contact with the agency.

9. Pretesting the Interview

Principles for pretesting interviews have been discussed in chapter 2. These can be directly applied to telephone interviews as well. In addition, one should get some idea as to how the interviewer's voice transmits over the telephone, whether words are distinguishable and clear, and whether interviewer instructions are non-ambiguous. Ideally, the schedule should be pretested with several former clients who are similar to those who are to be included in the follow-up survey.

10. Preparing for Data Collection

Prior to the conduct of the telephone interview, potential respondents should be apprised that they may be called. This can be done routinely during the final treatment session, or it can be done by letter. Finally, a short telephone call might be used to inform the former client that a telephone interview will be forthcoming. Under certain circumstances, one might want to send the interviewee a copy of the interview schedule in advance of the interview. In addition a specific day, date and time might be set up for the interview. All of these techniques help to increase the rate of response and decrease the ultimate cost of the study.

11. Implementing Data-Collection Procedures

In implementing the actual interviews, it is important for the interviewer to distinguish the information gathering process from therapeutic interviewing. This is especially important if the interviewer is the person who provided treatment in the past. If the former client is again in need of treatment, appointments can be made after the follow-up interview is completed. Hence, it should be made clear to the respondent that treatment is not the *primary* purpose of the interview. Finally, it is important to check for completion of questions by all respondents. If there are questions which tend to go unanswered, the interview schedule has not been adequately pretested and refined. These questions, then, become useless sources of information.

12. Tabulating and Analyzing Data

Using the principles described in the previous chapter, data should then be aggregated and analyzed in relation to the primary purpose of the follow-up study. Frequency of response and percentages of former clients who respond to various alternatives should be tabulated for closed-ended questions. If there are relatively large numbers of respondents (say more than 50) it might be possible to cross-tabulate interviewee responses with other important variables such as age, gender, social class, and so on.

HYPOTHETICAL ILLUSTRATION

A community mental health worker has decided to conduct a follow-up survey of clients s/he has treated during the past year. Of the 200 clients seen, most were treated for problems defined as anxiety, depression, and/or situational reactions.

1. Defining the Purpose of the Survey

The purpose of the study is to determine whether former clients have maintained their progress after treatment has been terminated and whether they were satisfied with the treatment they did receive. Moreover, the social worker is interested in whether these people have recently received treatment elsewhere and whether or not they would return to the agency if the original problem recurred or if new problems arose.

2. Identifying the Target Population and the Sampling Unit

The social worker determines that s/he can interview by phone about 80 former clients in the two-week period set aside for the study. Of the 200 clients seen, 160 were terminated after a full course of treatment. These represent the target population for the study. Each such former client then will represent a sampling unit for the study.

3, 4, 5. Determining Sampling Procedures

Since the social worker does not have time to interview all 160 former clients, a 50 percent sample is required. A systematic sampling strategy with a sampling ratio of 1:2 is chosen. The target population is then listed alphabetically and after a random starting point, every other case is chosen for a follow-up interview.

6. Checking the Representativeness of the Sample

After the sample has been selected, comparisons are made between the target population and the sample on characteristics such as gender, race, age, and problem definition. Percentage comparisons and chi-squares indicate that on these dimensions there are no statistically significant differences between sample and target populations.

7 and 8. Constructing the Interview Schedule

The social worker then constructs the following interview schedule.

Introduction

Hello _____. This is _____ calling from the Midtown Community Mental Health Center. As I told you when we last saw each other, I might be phoning to obtain some information from you and from other former clients that I've seen. This interview should take no longer than 15 minutes. Is this a convenient time to talk to me? (If "no") When would be a more convenient time? (set up time) (If "yes"), Good, thanks for your time. The reason I'm interested in talking to you is so I can get some idea about how you are doing and how satisfied you were with the services you received from our agency. Naturally, your responses will be confidential and will not affect any future service requests you might make. Incidentally, if you do wish to resume treatment, time will be available at the end of the interview to discuss that. Shall we begin?

Interview Schedule

First, I'd like to ask some questions about the treatment you received.

1. Would you say that your treatment ended too soon, ended at just the right time, or should have ended sooner?

   too soon _____ right time _____ should have ended sooner _____

2. How satisfied were you with the treatment you did receive? Would you say you were: very satisfied _____ somewhat satisfied _____ somewhat dissatisfied _____ very dissatisfied _____

3. (If "somewhat" or "very dissatisfied" in above) Would you have preferred to have some other form of treatment? Yes _____ No _____

4. (If "yes") Can you tell me what that would be? _____

   _____

   _____

5. Overall, how successful do you think we were in solving the problems for which you entered treatment: Would you say we were: very successful _____ somewhat successful _____ somewhat unsuccessful _____ very unsuccessful _____

I see, now I'd like to ask some questions about how you've been doing since treatment ended.

6. In thinking about the problems that brought you into treatment, would you say that since treatment ended you've: continued to make progress _____ remained about the same _____ gotten worse _____

7. Compared to how you felt when treatment ended, would you say you are: more depressed _____ about the same _____ less depressed _____

8. Again, comparing yourself now with when you ended treatment, would you say you are: more anxious _____ about the same _____ less anxious _____

9. Since you ended treatment with this agency, have you received any help with mental health problems from any other social agencies? yes _____ no _____

10 . (If "yes") Would you describe the kind of help you received? _____
_____

b. From what agency did you receive this help? _____
_____

c. How helpful was it? very helpful _____ somewhat helpful _____ not helpful _____

11. Are you currently employed? yes _____ no _____ (If "yes") Where are you working and what do you do there?_____
_____

12. Do you attend school or take any training courses currently? yes _____ no _____ (If "yes") Where and what courses are you taking? _____
_____

13. Are there any problems which you now have for which you believe you need treatment? yes _____ no _____

14. (If "yes") Would you describe these problems?_____
_____

Would you like to set an appointment to come into the agency? yes _____ no _____ Appointment Time _____

15. Finally, are there any comments that you'd like to make about your progress or the services you've received from this agency? _____

Closing

Again, thank you very much for your time. This has been very helpful.

9. Pretesting the Interview

The interview is then pretested on three former clients not included in the sample, but drawn from the target population. Questions which seem to be difficult for the respondent to understand are reworded. It is found that the questionnaire is completed well within the 15-minute upper limit. On two out of three pretests, however, it was clear that the respondents were surprised to receive the phone call, indicating that they did not remember being told that they might receive a follow-up telephone interview when their treatment terminated. As a result, a decision is made to send those in the sample a letter telling them that they would be receiving a phone call, describing the purpose of the study and soliciting their cooperation.

10. Preparing for Data Collection

The social worker then reviews the case summary for each client in the sample, extracting information about the client's age, race, gender, employment status, marital status, and problem definition. These data are attached to the interview schedule that will be used in interviewing each former client. In addition, a letter is sent to all those in the sample population informing them that they will be called.

11. Implementing Data-Collection Procedures

Letters are then sent out. These are followed by telephone interviews. In those few cases in which former clients refuse to participate, they are asked why. This information might give some indication of their general attitude toward the agency and the social worker. In addition, clients who are not reached during the day, are called in the evening. Finally, those former clients who refuse to participate or who cannot be reached are replaced by others who are randomly selected from the remaining members of the target population. If, however, a sizable proportion (say more than 25 percent) refuse to participate, some analysis of the differences between respondents and nonrespondents should be attempted.

12. Analysis

After the interviews have been completed, the responses of former clients to closed-ended questions are then aggregated and placed in percentage form in the appropriate categories of a blank copy of the interview schedule. Open-ended responses are then analyzed by developing mutually exclusive and exhaustive code categories for these responses and filling in the percentages of responses which fall into each of these categories.

If the findings of the follow-up study show an increase in depression or anxiety after treatment, the social worker would wish to consider whether criteria used in terminating treatment should be revised. Cross-tabulations with background characteristics might be employed to determine whether some groups (say men versus women) seem to be doing better. In addition, it might become apparent that some groups tend to indicate that they should have been terminated sooner, whereas others may feel just the opposite. Finally, the extent to which former clients take their problems elsewhere may be seen as a serious negative indicator of satisfaction and effectiveness and would suggest some major changes in treatment method.

EXERCISE

Develop a follow-up survey for clients that you have treated in the past year. Determine whether sampling procedures will be necessary. If so, draw a sample and determine how representative it is.

Implement the survey. Describe the findings of the study. What are the implications of the study for your practice?

SELECTED BIBLIOGRAPHY

Babbie, Earl R., *Survey Research Methods* (Belmont, Calif.: Wadsworth, 1973), pp. 73–113, and 171–85.

Blalock, Jr., Hubert M., *Social Statistics* (New York: McGraw-Hill, 1960), pp. 212–21, 437, and 452.

Denzin, Norman K., *The Research Act* (2d ed.; New York: McGraw-Hill, 1978), pp. 157–81.

Dillman, Don A., *Mail and Telephone Surveys* (New York: Wiley, 1978), pp. 39–78, 200–81.

Goldstein, Harris K., *Research Standards and Methods for Social Workers* (New Orleans: Hauser Press, 1963), pp. 135–42.

Isaac, Stephen and William B. Michael, *Handbook in Research and Evaluation* (San Diego, Calif.: Robert R. Knapp, 1971), pp. 92–99.

Jenkins, Shirley, "Collecting Data by Questionnaires and Interview," in Norman A. Polansky, ed., *Social Work Research* (2d ed.; Chicago: University of Chicago Press, 1975), pp. 131–53.

Kadushin, Alfred, *The Social Work Interview* (New York: Columbia University Press, 1972), pp 7–23 and 105–40.

Sudman, Seymour, *Reducing the Cost of Surveys* (Chicago: Aldine, 1967), pp. 1–5 and 41–67.

Walker, Helen M. and Joseph Lev, *Statistical Inference* (New York: Holt, 1953), pp. 261–88.

10

THE USE OF RATING SCALES IN BEFORE/AFTER EVALUATIONS

Follow-up evaluations, discussed in chapter 9, are often referred to as after-only evaluations because they rely completely on data collected after treatment has been terminated. And, as we indicated earlier, while these types of formative evaluations are relatively easy to implement, they shed little light on the extent to which the client has changed during the treatment process.

Before/after or *pretest/post-test* evaluation designs are slightly more refined than after-only designs in that the former designs rely on measurements taken before treatment has begun *and* after it has been terminated. Differences between these sets of measurements are then attributed to the treatment received. Although this somewhat more complex formative design does not provide direct information about what would happen if clients received no treatment, it is a methodological improvement over follow-up evaluations, indicating the extent to which treatment and client change are associated. In other words, it shows whether or not the client has changed along specified dimensions over the time in which treatment took place.

To make valid before/after comparisons, however, requires valid and reliable rating scales which can be used to measure treatment effectiveness. Such scales can be used to rate client attitudes, behaviors, or mood states. They can be numerical or verbal. The ratings themselves can be client self-assessments, the assessments of significant others in the client's environment, or the assessment of the clinician.

Numerous types of rating scales appear in the social science literature. A *Likert scale* is one in which the rater is asked to indicate the extent of agreement, ranging from "strongly agree" to "strongly disagree," with a set of statements. By tallying the number of agreements with statements which reflect a given attitudinal dimension, one can rate individual respondents according to where they place on that dimension. These scales are relatively easy to construct and can be used quite effectively by nonresearch specialists.

More complex scaling techniques have been authored by Thurstone and by Guttman. A *Thurstone scale* involves placing an individual along a numerical continuum which represents an attitudinal or behavioral dimension. Each interval on this scale is presumed to be equivalent, so that on a depression scale of 1 to 10, a rating of 4 is treated as though it indicates twice the amount of depression as would a rating of 2, and half the amount of depression as would a rating of 8.

A *Guttman scale* consists of a set of items or statements that form a continuum in themselves. These statements are usually responded to with agree/disagree responses. Since the statements themselves vary in intensity along a continuum, it is possible to place the individual respondent by determining the most extreme statement with which s/he would agree. Thus, a Guttman scale of optimism about the future would involve statements that were increasingly optimistic. One would determine how optimistic a respondent is by determining what is the most optimistic statement with which the respondent would agree.

Thurstone and Guttman scales involve some rather complex techniques that render them impractical for clinical social workers to construct. In addition, they require a great deal of time to perfect and sophisticated techniques to analyze. However, for those interested in a detailed discussion of these scaling techniques, see Shaw and Wright (1967).

Some social scientists have devoted their attention to the development of scales which directly measure treatment effectiveness. Examples of such goal-attainment scaling systems are provided by Kiresuk and Sherman (1968) and by Ellis and Wilson (1973). The former involves rating treatment efficacy directly on a scale from −2, which means the "most unfavorable treatment outcome thought likely" to +2, which stands for the "best anticipated success with the treatment." The latter scale rates treatment effectiveness from 1 to 6, with a score of 1, indicating that the client was "much further from" the treatment goals after treatment was completed to a score of 6, which indicates "sufficient attainment" of treatment goals.

While the foregoing measures of goal-attainment are useful in follow-up evaluations, they do not lend themselves to before/after studies. In these evaluations, measures of the severity of symptoms are likely to be used. Thus, for example, Honigfeld and Klein (1973) have constructed a scale that ranges from 1 (which indicates "absence of symptoms") to 7 (which indicates "severe symptoms"). Applying this scale to a dimension such as paranoia one might rate a client before and after treatment. By comparing the two scores, an indirect measure of treatment success or failure is obtained.

RATING SCALES AND CLINICAL PRACTICE

Rating scales can be used in each stage of clinical social work practice. Thus, for example, in diagnostic assessment the Honigfeld and Klein scale described above can be used to rate the severity of a client's symptomatology on any number of psychosocial dimensions.

During treatment implementation, rating scales can be used to assess the extent to which individual clinicians are conforming to professional standards of treatment. Many quality assurance assessment instruments include such scales.

Finally, rating scales are useful in measuring treatment outcomes. These scales may be original scales, devised by an individual clinician to measure the highly specific changes in an individual client in the course of treatment. Or, they may be already available and highly standardized measures which have been used with large numbers of clients in numerous treatment programs.

Here we describe the use of rating scales in before/after studies with individual clients and aggregates of clients. In this context, a number of existing scales are referred to and the principles for applying them are discussed. Finally, using the versatile chi-square again, we demonstrate how the statistical significance of client change can be assessed.

PRINCIPLES FOR USING RATING SCALES

1. Specifying Treatment Objectives

To employ rating scales in assessing the effectiveness of treatment, one begins by specifying treatment objectives. In addition, one should estimate when these changes in client attitudes, behaviors, moods or relationships are expected to take place. This process of specification should routinely take place during the treatment planning phase and before treatment implementation. It may involve social worker and client jointly or the social worker alone.

Once the broad dimensions of treatment effectiveness are identified, they need to be operationally defined, that is translated into measurable terms. Thus, for example, treatment may have as its purpose the reduction of anxiety in a given client. This broad treatment goal might be measured in a number of ways: client sleep patterns, frequency of digestive problems, client perception of anxiety, worker perception of client anxiety during treatment, and so on. Ideally, more than one operational definition or measurable index will be identified for each broad treatment objective. However, since data will have to be collected for each of these effectiveness measures, there should not be so many that the collection of the data intrudes on the treatment process.

In addition to specifying treatment objectives, one should probably identify any possible negative outcomes that might result during treatment. "Symptom substitution" measures of other symptoms may accompany client improvement; hence, a client who is treated for anorexia might develop other eating or physical disturbances as the anorexia abates. An individual in conjoint therapy might experience unspecified feelings of anxiety with increased leisure time spent with his or her spouse. Whenever possible, such undesirable outcomes should be anticipated and built into measurement instruments.

Finally, it should be remembered that in before/after studies, measures of effectiveness must remain exactly the same before and after treatment. Thus, to document change the before and after measures must be exactly alike. Any new measures added after treatment has been completed can only be used as follow-up or after-only measures. This means that in before/after studies a good deal more attention must be given to measures of effectiveness earlier in the treatment process than is the case in follow-up studies.

2. Determining Whether Existing Rating Scales Can be Used

As we indicated in chapter 3 existing rating scales can be located in professional journals, compendia of research instruments, research institutions, and so on. The principles for locating client assessment instruments described in that chapter can be easily applied to locating treatment effectiveness scales and measuring client change. Whenever possible, existing scales should be used. Examples of some available sources of scales relevant to measuring treatment effectiveness are as follows (complete references are in the bibliography at the end of the chapter):

1. Ellsworth (1975) has developed three forms of a Personal Adjustment and Role Skill Scale (PARS) that can be filled out by friends, relatives or half-way house residential care personnel in rating the community adjustment of former mental patients and in rating the effectiveness of mental hospital programs.
2. Kiresuk and Sherman (1968) offer basic procedures for developing goal-attainment scales that can be used in a variety of social agency contexts.
3. Lyerly and Abbott (1966) present a number of scales for rat-

ing the social adjustment and symptomatology of psychiatric patients.

4. Shaw and Wright (1967) discuss an array of attitude rating scales useful in such diverse contexts as probation, employment, and so on.

Existing scales can be used directly, or they may serve to suggest component items or questions, or response system formats for original scales constructed by the clinician to suit a particular situation. For example, the response categories in an existing goal-attainment scale may be linked to treatment goals which are unique to a particular client or set of clients.

3. Determining Who Is To Do the Ratings

Rating effectiveness can be done by the clinician, the client, or significant others in the client's life. The determination of who should do the actual rating would depend on the potential for objectivity, access to the client, time available, and so on. Ideally, of course, it would be better if more than one person rated the client. This would promote greater confidence in the ratings.

Another factor which affects the reliability of the ratings is the extent to which the rater understands the dimensions covered in the scale and the system for recording observations or perceptions. When the clinician is not doing the rating, s/he should take the time to fully explain the use of the scale to those who are doing the actual rating. Moreover, the social worker should make at least an informal assessment of the degree to which his/her clinical observations of the client are consistent with the ratings provided by the client or significant others. Calling attention to such inconsistencies may provide useful clinical material as well as clarify the client's present condition.

A final consideration in selecting the rater, is the conditions under which the rating will take place. As much as possible, the conditions under which the ratings are made should be standardized. Thus, the person doing the rating should be able to observe the client in regular intervals, in similar situations, which are relevant to the goals of treatment. Thus, a child in treatment for learning problems, should probably be rated by his/her teacher. Mood states are probably most accurately assessed by the client him/herself. Whoever is doing the rating, should be carefully instructed as to when and under what conditions ratings should be made.

4. Constructing Stimulus and Response Systems for Rating Scales

In rating scales, the *stimulus* refers to the question, set of instructions, or statements to which the rater is supposed to respond. Stimuli can take the form of narratives which describe sets of behaviors, single sentences, phrases, words or questions. *Response systems* represent the formats within which the ratings are made. They are similar to the response systems in closed ended questions. In the scale below, "severity of depression" is the stimulus, and the numbers 1 through 9 are the response categories. The statements under scale steps 1, 3, 5, 7, and 9 are referred to as *anchoring* illustrations. They promote the reliability of the ratings.

Severity of Depression

1	2	3	4	5	6	7	8	9

Not Depressed	Slightly Depressed	Moderately Depressed	Strongly Depressed	Severely Depressed

Note that as with closed-ended questionnaire items, the response categories are mutually exclusive and exhaustive. Below are some possible stimuli and response systems for rating a client's level of anxiety:

(1) *Presence/Absence of Symptom*
    appearance of anxiety

    0—absent
    1—present

(2) *Adverbial Scales of Frequency of Symptom*
    How often is the client anxious?

    1—very infrequently
    2—infrequently
    3—frequently
    4—very frequently

(3) *Adverbial Scales of Severity of Symptom*

How anxious is the client?

1—not at all anxious
2—slightly anxious
3—moderately anxious
4—strongly anxious
5—severely anxious

(4) *Frequency Scales By Percentage*

About what percentage of the time is the client anxious?

0—0%
1—1–10%
2—11–20%
3—21–30%
4—31–40%
5—41–50%
6—51–60%
7—61–70%
8—71–80%
9—81–90%
10—91–100%

(5) *Frequency Designated By Time Intervals*

About how often does the client appear anxious?

1—once a month or less
2—once every two weeks
3—once a week
4—twice a week
5—every other day
6—daily

(6) *Likert Scale (with or without neutral category)*

The client appears anxious.

1—strongly agree
2—agree
3—uncertain
4—disagree
5—strongly disagree
          or
1—strongly agree
2—agree

3—disagree
4—strongly disagree

(7) *Bipolar Scale*

On a scale from 1 to 7 rate the client from calm to anxious.

1	2	3	4	5	6	7

very calm	neither calm nor anxious	very anxious

(8) *Comparative Scales*

Compared to when the client began treatment, which would you say s/he is now?

1—much more anxious
2—more anxious
3—about the same
4—less anxious
5—much less anxious

(9) *Goal Attainment Scales*

To what extent has the client achieved the objective of reducing his/her anxiety?

+2—client is completely free of anxiety. The goal is fully achieved

+1—client has occasional episodes of anxiety, but these do not interfere with social functioning

0—client has episodes of anxiety which occasionally interfere with social functioning

−1—client has frequent episodes of anxiety which interfere with social functioning

−2—client is anxious most of the time and does not function socially; treatment does not appear to have had any impact on his/her anxiety

The foregoing scales are only a sampling of those available. In choosing or constructing a scale, the following principles should be kept in mind:

1. Avoid having too many or too few scale points. Too many scale points could lead to unreliability in the ratings. Too few could lead to a lack of discrimination of important differences. Typically, scales have 4 or 5 steps in them.

2. Provide anchoring illustrations for several scale points, especially the ends and the middle of the scale. These promote inter-rater reliability.

3. When several different dimensions of client behavior are being rated, use only a few response systems. The greater the number of response systems used, the greater the likelihood of response error. Moreover, having to follow many different response systems may lead to respondent fatigue.

4. In attempting to measure a concept that has several component dimensions, one should use several subscales to measure these different dimensions. Thus, for example, the concept of "social adjustment" may involve attitudes toward work, family, community, and so on. Each of these dimensions can be measured with a separate subscale. And, an overall measure of social adjustment can be arrived at by adding the individual's score on the respective subscales. To correctly perform this data manipulation, each subscale must have the same response system and each set of responses must be scored the same way. So, if there are three component subscales, each with three stimulus items, each scoring from 1 (low adjustment) to 5 (high adjustment), by adding the scores for all the items one can compute an overall score of social adjustment. This is called a *cumulative* or *additive index* of social adjustment. On this index, any individual can range from a score of 9 (which would indicate the lowest social adjustment possible) to a score of 45 (which would indicate the highest adjustment possible).

5. Minimizing Bias in the Stimulus and Response Systems

Stimulus errors are those scoring errors which result from bias in the wording of the characteristic to be assessed or in the instructions given to the rater. These errors can be minimized by clear, unambiguous instructions and by avoiding value-laden terms in the stimulus items themselves. In addition, outside raters should be assured that accuracy is more important than pleasing the clinician or the client. When the client or clinician is doing the rating, each must approach this task with complete honesty. Naturally, for this to be accomplished the client-rater must be rewarded by the clinician for honesty, just as the clinician-rater must be rewarded by his/her agency. It is pointless to attempt to evaluate treatment if only positive outcomes are rewarded and negative outcomes punished.

Response errors are those errors in scoring which arise from biased response systems. There are a number of different types of response errors which the scale constructor should keep in mind. These are errors which result from: unbalanced scales, halo effects, the avoidance of extreme scale points, and central tendency effects.

Unbalanced scales are those in which the response categories are more heavily weighted in one direction or another. Thus, a 4-point scale of therapeutic progress which ranges from 1 (a small amount of progress) to 4 (a great amount of progress) would not entertain the possibility that the client makes no progress or even gets worse during treatment. A more balanced and less biased scale would provide an equal number of categories for these less desirable outcomes.

Halo effects are response errors which result when the response to one scale or scale item is affected by responses to previous scales or scale items. This is most likely to occur when a series of nonspecific and socially desirable traits are being rated such as trustworthiness, helpfulness, kindness, and the like. Scoring an individual high on one is likely to lead to high scores on subsequent dimensions. Halo effects cannot be completely eliminated, but they can be minimized. This is accomplished by varying response systems, by occasionally reversing positive and negative ends of bipolar rating scales, and by stimulus items which are sometimes positive and sometimes negative. The order of these variations in items should be random. In following these procedures, however, one must be careful to take into account these scoring reversals in accumulating or interpreting scores.

Thus, in our earlier social adjustment index, if adjustment to work and community subscale are scored from 1 (low adjustment) to 5 (high adjustment) and are to be combined with a scale of maladjustment within the family which is scored from 1 (low maladjustment) to 5 (high maladjustment), the values of the scores of the family subscale would have to be reversed ($5 = 1$, $4 = 2$, and so on) for it to be added to the other two subscales. Failure to pay meticulous attention to the directionality of the scoring systems can obviously lead to considerable error in computation and interpretation.

Central tendency errors are those which result from the raters consistently choosing non-committal, neutral or middle points on rating scales. These errors can be minimized by response systems which do not have "neutral" or "undecided" response categories or by increasing the number of response categories which are close to neutral. Thus, depending on the situation, a cruder or a more refined scale may be called for when ratings are consistently non-committal.

A similar type of error results when respondents give relatively noncommittal responses to *avoid extreme alternatives*. Thus, a scale which has three points on it—"always," "sometimes," and "never"—is likely to generate a high proportion of "sometimes" responses irrespective of the attitude, mood, or behavior that is being rated. Here, more refined categories between sometimes and the two extremes would be called for.

6. Writing Instructions

In constructing scales, instructions should be provided to the rater which specifically tell the rater how to indicate which rating is being given for each item. Statements such as "circle one," "check one," and "write in the number which comes closest to your opinion," should accompany each set of stimuli or response systems. Included in the introduction to a set of items might be the definitions of the scaler dimensions, the information to be used in making the ratings, and the information that should be excluded from consideration.

7. *Pretesting and Implementing the Rating Scales*

Just as with other research instruments, rating scales should be pretested before they are actually implemented. Pretesting should focus on the clarity of instructions, the feasibility of actually doing the ratings, the degree to which the rating scales yield an appropriate amount of internal variation (a treatment progress scale on which all clients are scoring high is not likely to be a useful scale), and inter-rater reliability, if more than one rater is being employed. Principles for pretesting observational instruments apply here (see chapter 4) as well.

Scales should be modified in accordance with the pretest findings. It is important to remember to pretest scales *with* those who are planning to employ them, *on* those who are as much like the clients to be rated as possible. If clients are not available for pretesting, role-playing can be usefully employed.

Once the scales have been pretested and modified, they are implemented before treatment begins and when treatment is terminated. As the scales are actually being implemented, however, care should be taken to standardize the conditions under which they are applied. If the clinician him/herself is doing the ratings, a colleague or supervisor may be used for checking the reliability of his/her ratings. Principles for testing inter-rater reliability apply here as they do during pretesting.

8. *Analyzing and Interpreting the Findings*

Effectiveness measures should be analyzed and interpreted in the light of the treatment goals upon which client and social worker agreed. In after-only studies they can tell us whether the client is functioning at a desired level when treatment is terminated. In before/after studies, the comparisons of ratings made before treatment began and after treatment terminated, can tell us something about how much the client changed during the course of treatment, as well as whether a desirable level of outcome has been achieved. Thus, before/after studies provide a more substantial basis for the inference that positive client functioning is associated with treatment than do after-only evaluations.

In before/after studies, one procedure that can be employed to assess client progress is to simply compare the before and after scores on each scalar dimension to determine whether the client has improved, remained the same, or gotten worse. When several scales or scale items (at least 20) have been used, an overall assessment of individual client change or nonchange can be determined by cross-tabulating all the before and after measures in one *contingency table*. The latter would be a 2×2 table in which four categories of client change or nonchange are recorded; that is, those scalar dimensions or items on which the client had desirable pretreatment scores and undesirable post-treatment scores, desirable pre- and post-treatment scores, undesirable pre- and post-treatment scores, and undesirable pre-treatment and desirable post-treatment scores. It would look something like table 10.1.

		Post-treatment Scores		
		Undesirable	*Desirable*	
Pre-treatment	*Desirable*	A	B	A + B
Scores	*Undesirable*	C	D	C + D
		A + C	B + D	N = A + B + C + D

TABLE 10.1

To construct it, one has to split each scalar response in two. This is done by determining the point on each scale that indicates an acceptable score. This can be based on the median response to the scale during pretesting or on *a priori* category labels. Scores of each scale are then collapsed into desirable (those at the acceptable level or above) and undesirable (those below the acceptable level). Using the same "cutting point" for a given scale on the pre- and post-treatment scores and aggregating all the scales, one can readily determine the number of scores that fall into each pre- and post-treatment category. These are the quantities that appear *outside* the table $(A + B, C + D, A + C, B + D)$. Then by ascertaining the number of scores that fall *inside* any one cell, one can easily derive the numbers in all the other cells. Finally, using the total number of scores as the percentage base $(A + B + C + D)$, one can determine the percentage of scores falling into each cell of the table.

Those dimensions recorded in cell A would indicate attributes on which the client had deteriorated in the course of treatment. Cell B, would indicate dimensions on which a client had maintained his/her pre- and post-treatment desirable attributes. Cell C would indicate dimensions on which a client had maintained pre-treatment undesirable attributes. And, cell D would indicate movement from undesirable to desirable scores during the course of treatment. Naturally, cells A and C are least favorable, and cells B and D most favorable.

To illustrate, let us consider a 20-item Likert scale of client anxiety. Clients are to indicate strong agreement, mild agreement, mild disagreement, or strong disagreement with twenty statements indicative of anxiety or of the absence of anxiety. This scale is administered to a client before treatment begins and when treatment terminates.

Once the pre- and post-treatment data have been collected, scores are collapsed into agree and disagree responses. Being careful to take into account the direction of the wording of each stimulus item, responses are then dichotomized into those indicating high anxiety versus those indicating its absence. Table 10.2 shows the pre- and post-treatment scores.

Table 10.2 shows that the client's pre-treatment responses were equally divided among low anxiety and high anxiety (10 versus 10, respectively) responses. After treatment, however, there are many fewer high anxiety responses (2 high versus 18 low anxiety responses). The contingency table is completed by observing the

		Post-treatment		
		High anxiety	Low Anxiety	
Pre-treatment	Low Anxiety			10
	High Anxiety			10
		2	18	20

TABLE 10.2

number of items on which the client seemed to go from a low anxiety response to a high anxiety response (Cell A). It is determined that this has happened on one item. By placing the 1 in Cell A, we can complete the rest of the cells of the table. The complete contingency table, then, would look like table 10.3.

		Post-treatment		
		High Anxiety	Low Anxiety	
Pre-treatment	Low Anxiety	1 (5%)	9 (45%)	10
	High Anxiety	1 (5%)	9 (45%)	10
		2	18	20 (100%)

TABLE 10.3

By percentaging against the base of 20, we determine that on 5 percent of the items, the client has gone from low anxiety to high anxiety; on 5 percent of the items, the client maintained a high anxiety response; on 45 percent of the items, the client maintained a low anxiety response; and, on 45 percent of the items, the client went from high anxiety to low anxiety. This clearly indicates treatment success as far as the client's depression is concerned.

A similar analysis could be envisioned with an aggregate of 20 treatment *cases* in which a single measure of anxiety or a cumulative index of anxiety was used. The table would then indicate the percentage of cases in which the various categories of client change or nonchange was evidenced.

Finally, it is possible to calculate the statistical significance of client changes which occurred by employing the *McNemar Test for the Significance of Changes* (Siegel 1956). This procedure makes use of the versatile chi-square statistic. Using the formula,

$$\chi^2 = \frac{(A-D)^2}{A+D},$$

where A represents the number of responses that change from positive to negative during treatment and D represents the number that change from negative to positive; and substituting the findings in our illustrative example:

$$\chi^2 = \frac{(1-9)^2}{(1+9)}$$
$$\chi^2 = \frac{64}{10}$$
$$\chi^2 = 6.4$$

For a 2×2 contingency table, any value of chi-square exceeding 3.84 would indicate that the changes recorded were statistically significant beyond the .05 level of probability.* Hence, it would be safe to infer that the positive changes in the client were not a product of chance, but were associated with the treatment the client received.

HYPOTHETICAL ILLUSTRATION

A medical social worker has decided to try a group approach to working with women who have recently undergone mastectomies as treatment for breast cancer. The primary objective of group

---

*In interpreting the chi-square, however, one should always take care to determine that the changes that did occur were in the desired direction. Thus, it would be possible to get the same value of chi-square if the findings of the table were reversed and the client moved from a state of low anxiety (18 low anxiety responses) to a state of high anxiety (10 high anxiety responses) during the course of treatment.

treatment is to reduce feelings of depression, worthlessness, and the like, and to promote post-operative adjustment to marriage, family, job, and social activities. In the course of a year s/he has worked with three groups, each comprised of ten former patients. At the end of the year s/he would like to assess the impact that group treatment has made on these thirty women and to compare the results of group treatment with an equal population of patients who have received individual casework treatment. A before/after comparative study of the two treatment types is planned.

1. Specifying Treatment Objectives

As indicated earlier, the primary objective of treatment is to reduce patients' feelings of depression and to promote adjustment to marital, familial, occupational and social roles. It is expected that these objectives will be reached in three months.

2. The Use of Existing Rating Scales

After perusing existing rating scales, the worker decides to borrow the depression rating system developed by Lyerly and Abbott (1966). This involves rating depression on a 4-point scale from 1 (depression absent) to 4 (severe depression).

3. Determining Who Is To Do the Rating

The social worker decides to rate each patient in an individual pre- and post-treatment interview. This is presumed to be the most efficient and valid basis for clinically rating the patient.

4. Constructing Stimulus and Response Systems for Rating Scales

In constructing the rating scales, the social worker adapts the Lyerly and Abbott response system to an interview situation in which s/he will be the rater. Symptoms of depression are those patient self-reports indicating feelings of depression, thoughts of suicide, unexplained weight loss, insomnia, and the like. Original measures of marital adjustment, occupational adjustment, and adjustment to other social roles are constructed.

5. Minimizing Bias

In constructing the rating scales, attempts are made to keep stimulus and response errors to a minimum. Wording of both stimulus and response systems is checked for bias and imbalance.

6. Writing Instructions

Rating scales are pretested on a subsample of five breast cancer patients. A ward nurse will be asked to rate the patients based on his/her own interviews with the patients. Instructions are written so that the ward nurse will base ratings on the same behavioral cues that the social worker uses in making his/her ratings.

7. Pretesting and Implementing the Rating Scales

Once a relatively high degree of reliability is established between the nurse's and the social worker's ratings, the social worker begins to interview potential mastectomy patients. Pre-operative ratings on the above-mentioned dimensions of depression and adjustment are recorded for all patients. Once it has been determined whether a patient has had a mastectomy or not, patients are randomly assigned to group or individual treatment. After three months of group or individual treatment, patients are again rated by the social worker in individual interviews.

8. Analyzing and Interpreting the Findings

An analysis of patient change within each type of treatment category indicates that each type experienced a statistically significant decrease in depression. On the other measures of social adjustment, however, those who received individual treatment showed statistically significant improvement in marital adjustment, whereas those in group treatment showed statistically significant improvement in familial and occupational adjustment.

Since group treatment is more efficient and less costly than casework, the social worker decides to continue the group treatment program, but to provide individual casework for patients who seem to be experiencing particular difficulty in their marital relationships.

EXERCISE

Select a client with whom you are currently working. Specify one or more treatment objectives and construct a rating scale for each. How reliable and unbiased are these scales? How would you use them to assess client change?

SELECTED BIBLIOGRAPHY

Ellis, Richard H. and Nancy C. Z. Wilson, "Evaluating Treatment Effectiveness Using a Goal-Oriented Progress Note," *Evaluation*, Special Monograph no. 1, 1973, pp. 6–11.

Ellsworth, Robert B., "Consumer Feedback in Measuring the Effectiveness of Mental Health Programs," in Marcia Guttentag and Elmer L. Struening, eds., *Handbook of Evaluation Research* (Beverly Hills, Calif.: Sage, 1975), 2:239–74.

Goldstein, Harris K., *Research Standards and Methods for Social Workers* (New Orleans, La.: Hauser Press, 1963), pp. 37–108.

Gottman, John M. and Sandra R. Leiblum, *How To Do Psychotherapy and How To Evaluate It* (New York: Holt, Rinehart, and Winston, 1974), pp. 54–56.

Honigfeld, Gilbert and Donald F. Klein, "The Hillside Hospital Patient Progress Record: Explorations in Clinical Management by Objective and Exception," *Evaluation*, Special Monograph no. 1, 1973, pp. 19–22.

Isaac, Stephen and William B. Michael, *Handbook in Research and Evaluation* (San Diego, Calif.: Robert R. Knapp, 1971), pp. 58, 100–5.

Kiresuk, Thomas J. and Robert E. Sherman, "Goal Attainment Scaling: A General Method for Evaluating Comprehensive Community Mental Health Programs," *Community Mental Health Journal* (1968), 4(6):443–53.

Lyerly, Samuel B. and Preston S. Abbott, *Handbook of Psychiatric Rating Scales*, Public Health Service Publication No. 1495 (Bethesda, Md.: National Institute of Mental Health, 1966), pp. 1–8.

Marsh, Jeanne C., "The Goal-Oriented Approach to Evaluation: Critique and Case Study from Drug Abuse Treatment," *Evaluation and Program Planning* (1978), 1(1):41–51.

Nunnally, Jum C. and William H. Wilson, "Method and Theory for Developing Measures in Evaluation Research," in Elmer L. Struening and Marcia Guttentag, eds., *Handbook of Evaluation Research* (Beverly Hills, Calif.: Sage Publications, 1975), 1:227–88.

Selltiz, Claire, Marie Jahoda, Morton Deutsch, and Stuart W. Cook, *Research Methods in Social Relations* (rev. ed.; New York: Holt, 1959), pp. 345–56.

Siegel, Sidney, *Nonparametric Statistics for the Behavioral Sciences* (New York: McGraw-Hill, 1956), pp. 63–67.

Shaw, Marvin E. and Jack M. Wright, *Scales for the Measurement of Attitudes* (New York: McGraw-Hill, 1967), pp. 15–33.

11

INTERRUPTED TIME-SERIES DESIGNS

In their classic monograph "Experimental and Quasi-Experimental Designs for Research," Campbell and Stanley (1963) identify eight factors that can jeopardize the validity of the findings of a research study. Applied to treatment evaluation, these are: (1) contemporary history—unanticipated events may occur while treatment is under way that change the character of the intervention, the client's situation, or the client him/herself; (2) maturation—during the course of treatment, clients may change simply as a function of time, developmental growth, fatigue, and so on; (3) initial measurement effects—the process of measurement itself might affect client outcomes; (4) instrumentation—unreliability over time due to lack of standardization of the measures of effectiveness used; (5) statistical regression—the tendency of individuals or groups chosen for treatment on the basis of extreme scores on some measure of pathology or need to "naturally" regress to a more average score in subsequent testing regardless of the effects of treatment; (6) selection—differences among individuals receiving treatment can yield misleading generalizations concerning the effects of treatment; (7) subject mortality—certain types of individuals may drop out of treatment in disproportionate numbers, creating misleading generalizations based on those who remain; and (8) interaction effects—the combined effects of any and all of the above factors may be mistaken for the effects or the noneffects of treatment.

Unfortunately, the designs presented in chapters 9 and 10—after-only, and before/after designs—do not take account of these threats to validity. The after-only design attempts to measure the effects of treatment after it has been terminated. No data are collected before treatment begins or during the treatment process itself. Only one measure is taken after treatment has ended. As a result, it is impossible to determine whether the client has, in fact, changed during the course of treatment or whether the presumed consequences of treatment persist over time.

In before/after studies, one measurement is taken before treatment begins and another after treatment has terminated. Changes in client scores are attributed to the effects of treatment. While this design is an improvement over follow-up studies, differences in pre- and post-treatment scores may be the result of the instability of the measuring instruments used rather than the actual effects of treatment. Moreover, only one post-treatment measure tells us nothing about the persistence of treatment outcomes.

A design that controls for measurement instability before, during and after intervention is the *interrupted time-series design*. In this design, a series of measurements is made *before* treatment begins on variables that the intervention is intended to influence. These measurements serve as a *baseline* against which measurements taken during and after treatment are compared. The series of measurements taken *during* intervention indicates the rate of improvement in the client who is receiving treatment and, possibly, the point at which treatment no longer seems to be having a beneficial effect. The series of measurements taken *after* treatment has terminated, indicates whether the beneficial effects of treatment are lasting.

Although the interrupted time-series design does not control for *all* factors affecting internal validity to which Campbell and Stanley referred, does not produce knowledge that is undisputably causal about the impact of treatment intervention, and does not produce findings that are immediately generalizable to other treatment cases, this design can generate knowledge that is highly informative about the impact of treatment on a given client. Moreover, such information can be aggregated with interrupted time-series data based on comparable interventions with comparable clients. This makes possible the evaluation of the impact of treatment on client groups, that is, program evaluation.

INTERRUPTED TIME-SERIES DESIGNS AND CLINICAL PRACTICE

Interrupted time-series designs provide systematic data concerning each phase of clinical social work practice. Such data may be generated through the use of forms, observational techniques, questionnaires, interviews, and so on. The data gatherer can be the client him/herself, the clinician or significant others.

In situations in which direct measurement is likely to be too intrusive or obstructive of treatment, data may be taken from agency archives. For example, schools routinely keep records on attendance, grades, and disciplinary actions for all students. Social agency case records often contain repeated indications of a client's social, psychological, and economic situation. These unobtrusive measures can also serve as a basis for a series of measurements before, during, and after treatment intervention.

In this chapter, the principles for implementing interrupted time-series designs are discussed. In this context, simple graphic and statistical techniques are described, which indicate whether client change observed during and after treatment is statistically significant. Interrupted time-series designs can be embellished in a number of ways to add to the refinement of the knowledge they produce. In the next chapter, some of these design refinements are discussed.

PRINCIPLES FOR IMPLEMENTING INTERRUPTED TIME-SERIES DESIGNS

1. Specifying Treatment Objectives

As with every other treatment evaluation design, interrupted time-series designs begin with specification of treatment objectives. The difference between interrupted time-series designs and those discussed earlier, however, is that in the former it is necessary to begin taking measurements on these objectives long before treatment begins. As a result, the specification and operationalization of treatment objectives must take place quite early in the clinical process. Thus, interrupted time series designs are best suited to treatment situations in which desired client outcomes are relatively standardized and easily identifiable such as in weight or smoking reduction, improving school attendance, and the like.

2. Operationally Defining Treatment Objectives

In interrupted time-series designs as with other treatment evaluation designs, treatment objectives should be operationally defined in a manner which is consistent with the client's understanding of the objectives of treatment. This is particularly important when the client is the data collector. Matching objectives to measures frequently presents a problem when the data are drawn from archival sources, for the clinician must rely upon the categories of information already available. Since this information was probably collected for other purposes, considerable ingenuity must be used sometimes to fit the categories of information that are available to the objectives of treatment.

As with other evaluation designs, measurement scales can be nominal, ordinal, or interval and should be subjected to tests of measurement reliability and validity (see earlier chapters on these subjects). However, for an interrupted time-series design, it is especially important that measures of treatment effectiveness have a high test/retest reliability (a correlation of at least .80) since the research design requires repeated use of the same measures. If test/retest reliability is low, it is impossible to determine whether fluctuations on the outcome measures are reflective of the impact of the treatment intervention or of the instability of the measuring device.

3. Specifying the Treatment Strategy

Once treatment objectives have been delineated and operationally defined, the treatment intervention should be specified. A complete and behaviorally specific description of the treatment strategy is necessary for monitoring whether the client is, in fact, receiving the intended intervention. Without this, it would be improper to infer that a particular intervention strategy was more or less effective. In other words, in order to test effectiveness of treatment, one must first determine that the client has received it.

Such specification of the treatment is also necessary if one intends to aggregate those cases that have been treated by a single social worker, and/or cases that have been treated by more than one worker. Aggregation requires comparable treatment means as well as comparable treatment objectives. In general, interrupted time-series designs work best when the treatment intervention itself can be standardized from session to session, from client to client, and from clinician to clinician.

Specification of the treatment strategy is also important in evaluating forms of treatment based on previous interrupted time-series studies. A new intervention may be shown to be much more effective than a previous approach, but if no effort is made to rigorously specify what the social worker did, the study is useless for describing and communicating the treatment innovation to others.

4. Taking Baseline Measurements

Prior to diagnostic assessment and treatment implementation, five or six measurements should be taken on the scales being used to assess client problems or treatment effectiveness. Such measures, taken at regular intervals before treatment begins are called *baseline measures*. So, for example, a caseworker working with a depressed patient on a hospital ward may observe the client at regular daily intervals for a week prior to initiating treatment. Should treatment be called for, the measures of depressed behavior would be recorded at similar intervals during treatment. After treatment, a follow-up evaluation would use the same intervals for determining whether treatment gains appear to persist.

Under certain circumstances, treatment begins with the first contact between client and social worker, and the foregoing mode of baselining may be impossible. In these instances, it may be possible to construct a baseline from archival data already available within the agency (for example, attendance records, medical reports, parole reports, and so on). Another possibility is to interview significant others in the client's environment to get an approximation of the frequency (relative to some standard time unit of problematic client behaviors, attitudes or moods.

When direct baselining is possible, an important consideration is when should repeat measures be taken. Unfortunately, there is no simple formula for this. Here again issues of validity, reliability, feasibility and cost enter in. It is a matter of judgment that depends on the variables to be measured, the intrusiveness of the measures, and the context within which measurement takes place. To monitor weight loss, weekly measures may suffice. For determining progress in resolving parent–child difficulties of some sort, daily measures of parent–child conflict may be necessary. Whatever the measurement interval, however, it is essential that baseline measures be taken at regular intervals and that the same intervals be used for measurement during and after treatment. This standardization of the application of the research instrument reduces the possibility that fluctuations in client scores are the consequence of different testing conditions.

5. Graphing the Baseline Data

Before treatment begins, one would want to establish a degree of stability in measures of client problems. If baseline stability is not established and treatment begins, natural fluctuations on these measures may be incorrectly interpreted as treatment outcomes. Graphing the baseline data helps us determine whether stability has been established.

A graph is a visual device for describing regularities and irregularities in the data over time. In a baseline graph, the horizontal axis is used to represent the time intervals between measurements. The vertical axis is used to represent either individual scores for one client or average scores for more than one client. A separate baseline graph should be constructed for each measure of client problem, or progress.

Stability is established when the line connecting the scores on a particular measure runs parallel to the horizontal axis (figure 11.1a); is not parallel, but maintains a constant angle or slope with the horizontal axis (figure 11.1b); or follows a regular and consistent pattern (figure 11.1c).

By "eyeballing" the baseline graph, one can get a sense of whether client scores are relatively high or low; increasing, decreasing, or constant; stable, cyclic, or totally unpredictable. It is important to keep in mind, however, that a graph is only a pictorial representation of client behavior, attitude or mood over time. And, by altering the physical properties of the graph itself, stable patterns can look unstable, high scores can look low, and so on. As a consequence, graphs should be constructed and interpreted in a manner which is consistent with common sense and practice experience. Overall, the essence of baseline stability is that it is predictable, not that it is the same from time interval to time interval.

6. *Assessing the Needs for Intervention*

Using the baseline for diagnostic purposes, there are three conditions under which intervention would not be necessary: (1) if the magnitude of the problem or the frequency of its appearance is not great enough to indicate that there is a serious persistent problem; (2) if the slope of the baseline indicates a rapid decline in the problem without treatment; (3) if group average scores obscure the fact that particular individuals in the group have no need for treatment.

FIGURE 11.1

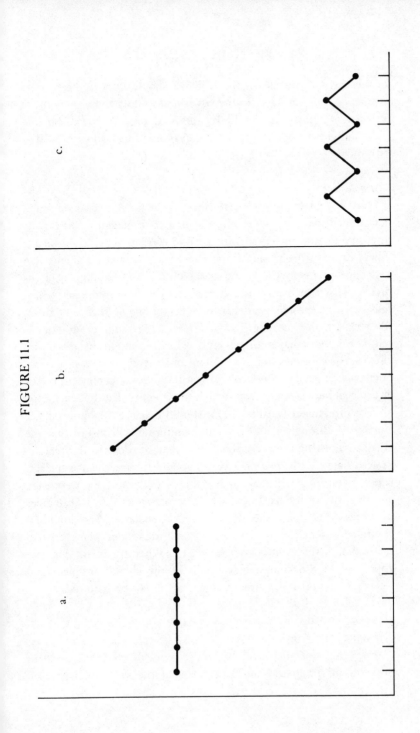

In the first two instances, the clinician should decline the request or referral for treatment. In the last instance, only those individuals in need of treatment should be required to participate. Sorting these individuals out would require examining individual as well as group baselines.

7. Implementing Treatment

Once a stable pattern is established in the baseline data, and it is determined that client problems occur with sufficient frequency or intensity to warrant clinical intervention, treatment should begin. The treatment itself, should be consistent with a treatment plan and appropriate to the client's problem. If the baseline data indicate that client problems are of a relatively low frequency or intensity, or the problems appear to be decreasing on their own or on the strength of the client's own efforts and resources, treatment might do more harm than good. Thus, it might heighten the client's consciousness of a problem and thereby increase its frequency. Or, it may interfere with natural internal coping processes or external help systems from which the client is already benefiting.

When treatment is called for, it should be closely monitored (see chapters 5 through 8). Treatment monitoring will insure that the client is receiving the prescribed treatment, at prescribed intervals, in accordance with treatment planning and the treatment contract. Close monitoring will make it possible to determine the frequency and intensity of the treatment which accompanies different degrees of success. In this monitoring process, the social worker should be continually sensitive to whether or not treatment plans are actualized and treatment goals are realistic. When treatment does not appear to be working, reassessment of the client's problem and reformulation of the treatment objectives might be required.

8. Taking a Series of Measures During Intervention To Evaluate Progress

From the time treatment begins, a series of measures of client problems or progress should be taken at the same intervals and with the same measures which were used for pre-treatment baselining. The purpose of such data is to determine whether progress is being made in relation to the treatment objectives. The use of the same measurement procedures reduces the chances that measured "effects" are the product of random errors in the measurement process and increases the chances that the findings during the treatment phase are truly reflective of client progress. For program evaluations, average scores for all those who received the treatment should be graphed.

9. Comparing Pre-Treatment Baseline with Client Progress During Treatment

The data collected during treatment should then be graphed alongside the baseline data. In this chart, the point at which treatment intervention began should be clearly discernible.

After pre-treatment and during treatment data have been graphed, the trend lines are compared visually. Is there a change in the magnitude of the client scores after intervention begins (figure 11.2a)? Is there a change in the slope of the scores after intervention begins (figure 11.2b)? Is there a change in the pattern of client scores (figure 11.2c)?

If changes are discernible by visual inspection of the graph, one should seek confirmation that the changes are not the result of chance variations, but are statistically significant. One simple technique for determining whether differences are likely to be statistically significant has been proposed by Gottman (Gottman and Leiblum 1974). This technique is only useful, however, when the data collected after intervention began do not indicate a continuation of the same trend line established prior to intervention.* For

---

* The procedure suggested by Gottman also rests on the assumption that the measurements taken at each interval are not influenced by previous measurements (that is, they are independent of each other) and that measurements are taken at randomly selected times. Since neither criterion is likely to be met in an interrupted time-series study, our use of the Gottman technique yields only an approximation to statistical significance.

FIGURE 11.2

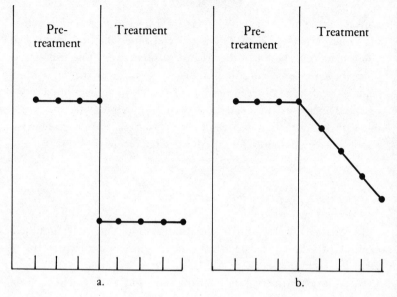

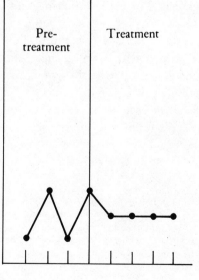

FIGURE 11.3

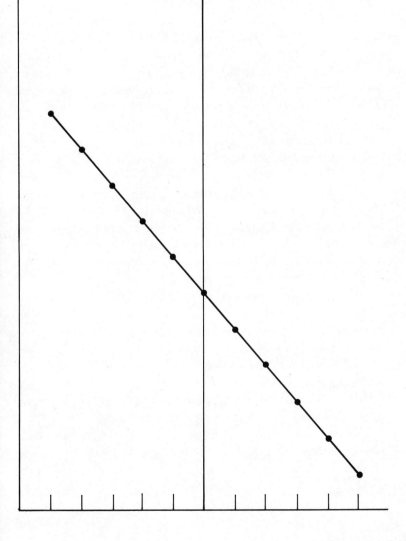

Pre-treatment   Treatment

example, the findings in figure 11.3 could not be used since they would give an erroneous impression of statistically significant progress when, in fact, the "effects" are not the result of treatment intervention. Thus, an inspection of the trend line in figure 11.3 strongly suggests that outcomes would have occurred without any intervention at all as a result of factors already operative during the pre-treatment phase.

To illustrate the process proposed by Gottman, consider the following example. A caseworker would like to systematically evaluate a new approach to counseling anorexic clients and their families. His/her goal is to stabilize a given client's weight, 20 pounds higher than it was when counseling began. Figure 11.4 represents the client's weight taken at weekly intervals before and during treatment.

Visual inspection of the graph reveals a cycle pre-treatment pattern and an overall increase in the client's weight after counseling began. In addition, there is some indication of weight stabilization in the last four weeks of treatment. To determine whether the client's progress is statistically significant: (1) calculate the mean for the baseline data; (2) draw a line parallel to the horizontal axis representing the mean for the baseline data; (3) calculate the standard deviation for the baseline data; (4) multiply the standard deviation by 2; (5) add this figure to the mean; (6) subtract it from the mean; (7) draw lines parallel to the horizontal axis, two standard deviations above and below the mean. If the measures taken during treatment fall outside these lines, it strongly suggests that the client's progress is statistically significant at the .05 level of probability. Finally, one should be sure to determine whether the statistically significant results are in the desired direction. Thus, they may indicate a statistically significant loss of weight during treatment. This would be a very serious outcome indeed.

Following the foregoing instructions in our example, we calculate the arithmetic mean of the baseline data ($\overline{X}$) by taking the sum of the weekly pre-treatment weights and dividing by the total number of weeks prior to intervention.

FIGURE 11.4

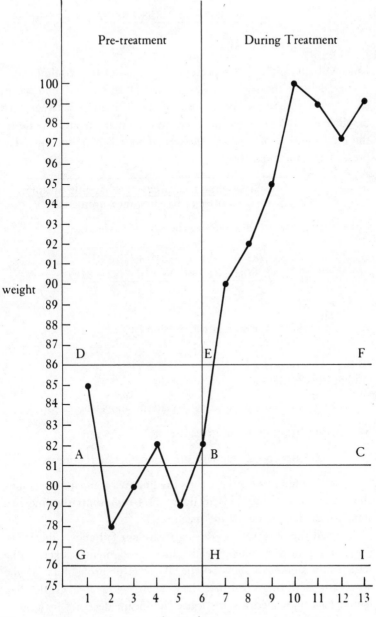

$$\overline{X} = \frac{85 + 78 + 80 + 82 + 79 + 82}{6}$$
$$\overline{X} = 81$$

Line ABC in figure 11.4 represents the mean of the baseline data.

To calculate the standard deviation (SD) of the baseline mean, we take the square root of the sum of the differences between each baseline measure and the baseline mean, square it and divide by the total number of baseline measurements taken, minus one. Expressed as a formula, this is:

$$SD = \sqrt{\sum \frac{(\text{each baseline measurement} - \text{baseline mean})^2}{\text{total number of baseline measurements} - 1}}$$

Substituting the baseline data in the formula, we get:

$$SD = \sqrt{\frac{(85 - 81)^2 + (78 - 81)^2 + (80 - 81)^2 + (82 - 81)^2 + (79 - 81)^2 + (82 - 81)^2}{6 - 1}}$$
$$SD = 2.5$$

We then multiply the standard deviation by 2:

$$2 \text{ SD} = 5.0$$

Adding this to the mean gives us:

$81 + 5.0 = 86 = 2$ standard deviations above the mean.

Subtracting from the mean gives us:

$81 - 5.0 = 76 = 2$ standard deviations below the mean.

Line DEF in figure 11.4 represents the line two standard deviations above the mean. Line GHI in figure 11.4 represents the line two standard deviations below the mean.

Since all the observations during treatment fall above line DEF, the increase in the client's weight during treatment is likely to be statistically significant beyond the .05 level of probability. If the observations during treatment had fallen below line GHI, they would have indicated a statistically significant decrease in weight.

Finally, if most of the observations during treatment had fallen between DEF and GHI, they would have indicated that the treatment was having no statistically significant impact on the client's weight.

Other, more complicated statistical techniques are suggested by Gottman and Leiblum (1974) and by Caporaso (1973). If the data do not lend themselves to a visual interpretation and to the simple statistical technique described above, a research consultant might be required to employ more complex tests of statistical significance.

Finally, if the social worker had been interested in evaluating the impact of treatment with several such clients, average weights of all the clients taken together would have served as the data base for the graph. To justify this, however, all clients would have had to receive the same diagnosis and the same treatment.

10. Collecting Supportive Data Regarding Contemporary History

Although the findings of interrupted time-series studies are not, strictly speaking, causal (this is largely because of the absence of control groups, or individuals who receive no treatment), there are ways to increase the certainty of the inferences drawn from these studies about the impact of treatment. This is done by collecting supportive evidence regarding the extent to which events external to the treatment might have accounted for client outcomes. Thus, one can rule out the effects of *multiple treatment interference* (Campbell and Stanley 1966) by determining whether the client has been simultaneously receiving other treatment for the problem from some other source. In addition, Carter (1972) suggests that questions can be asked about what other events in the client's life have been concurrent with treatment. Thus, situational factors, informal help sources, and the like must be ruled out to justify inferring more than a correlational connection between treatment and client outcomes. Once these steps have been taken, the interrupted time-series study can be said to provide an approximation of cause-effect knowledge.

11. Taking Post-Treatment Measures

When treatment gains have been stabilized at an acceptable level, treatment should be terminated. However, interrupted time-series designs require that a series of follow-up measures be taken post-intervention to determine whether treatment gains persist without further intervention. Here again, the same measures and measurement procedures are used to insure that post-intervention fluctuations are not the result of random errors in the measurement process.

12. Comparing Client Scores During and After Treatment

To systematically compare post-treatment scores with those collected during treatment, the original graph should be extended to include post-intervention data. A visual interpretation of the graph will indicate whether treatment gains have increased, maintained at the level attained during treatment, or declined. If they have declined, the clinician would want to know whether this decline is a statistically significant one. The statistical significance of the decline can be approximated by following procedures described earlier in this chapter. In this instance, however, the data collected *during* intervention serve as a "baseline" for computing the mean, the standard deviation, and so on. The follow-up data are then located within or outside the lines that represent two standard deviations above and below the mean of the client scores *during* treatment. If the follow-up scores generally fall within these lines, they would indicate that no statistically significant decline has taken place and that the client's weight has stabilized. If the follow-up scores fall below the lines, a statistically significant weight loss has occurred since treatment terminated and treatment would be offered again to the client. If follow-up scores fall above the lines, indicating a statistically significant weight increase, it might suggest that the client has gone on an eating binge and is not in control of his/her weight. Here again, treatment would be offered again.

Additional supportive data concerning "contemporary history

during post-treatment" might be collected here as well. This would help explain any unexpected changes after treatment has ended. Moreover, it can tell us something about the conditions under which stabilization of treatment gains takes place.

13. Comparing Client Scores From Each Clinical Phase

We have described three sets of data: (1) pre-treatment data; (2) data derived during treatment; and (3) post-treatment data. A complete interrupted time-series study would involve statistical comparisons of all three. Thus, a comparison of (1) and (2) would indicate whether treatment gains during treatment were statistically significant improvements over the pre-treatment phase. A comparison of (2) and (3) would indicate whether there have been statistically significant changes after treatment has terminated as compared with the levels reached during treatment. Finally, a comparison of (1) and (3) would indicate whether there was a statistically significant difference between the client's condition prior to treatment and his/her condition after treatment has been terminated.

Whatever the outcomes, however, it is important to remind the reader that their interpretation should not be purely mechanical and based on the statistics alone. They should be considered in the light of the clinician's common sense and practice experience. They should be compared with colleague's experiences with similar clients and similar courses of treatment. And, finally, they should be evaluated in relation to research and practice literature (see chapter 3).

HYPOTHETICAL ILLUSTRATION

A school social worker would like to try a group treatment approach with school phobic children. S/he identifies ten children, between the ages of eight and ten who have consistently poor attendance records, no serious medical or learning problems, and whose parents have indicated that their children are fearful of coming to school, complain of frequent headaches, stomach aches, and so on.

1. Specifying Treatment Objective

S/he begins by choosing as her/his treatment objective the reduction of the youngster's fears of school.

2. Operationally Defining Treatment Objective

The school social worker's operational definition of the treatment goal is to achieve and maintain a statistically significant improvement in the mean attendance scores of these youngsters within a two-month period.

3. Specifying the Treatment Strategy

A group treatment technique is formulated based on a review of recent literature and a training workshop in which the social worker was recently engaged. Treatment will occur on a weekly basis, on the same day and time each week. An appropriate time has been negotiated with the teachers of these children.

4. Taking Baseline Measures

Baseline measures of weekly attendance for the past two months are taken for each youngster and for the group as a whole. All but one of the ten children show remarkable regularity in their absence rates. The one child who does not, appears to be improving each week as the school year progresses. This child is not included in the treatment group and a new baseline is computed for the group based on the attendance of the nine remaining children.

5. Graphing the Baseline Data

Ten baseline graphs are constructed, one for each child in the treatment group, and one for the group of nine as a whole. The latter is based on the average attendance of the nine youngsters prior to treatment.

6 and 7. Implementing Treatment

Having established a need for treatment prior to inception of the program, the social worker begins his/her weekly sessions with the

12

VARIATIONS AND REPLICATIONS OF INTERRUPTED TIME-SERIES DESIGNS

In recent years, the interrupted time-series design has emerged as the basic paradigm for evaluative research in clinical social work practice. Starting with this design, clinical researchers have added a number of refinements and innovations which improve on the original. Together with replication studies, these design refinements and innovations produce knowledge which offers greater certainty about causal connections between clinical interventions and clinical outcomes.

We briefly describe three of these design variations, their uses, and their limitations. These are the graduated design, the withdrawal design, and the multiple baseline design. In addition, we discuss the importance of replicating interrupted time-series studies. Each of these evaluative approaches is based on the interrupted time-series format detailed in chapter 11. As a result, we will not be describing in detail the step-by-step principles for their implementation. More extensive and detailed discussions of these and

children. A detailed log is kept describing the techniques used each week, discussion topics, and so on, as well as the social worker's general impressions of how the youngsters are responding to these. Attention is given to which techniques and topics of discussion seem to be most successful in generating group participation.

8. Taking Measures During Treatment

Weekly attendance records are then added to the pre-treatment graphs for the two-month treatment period. This is done for each of the nine participants and for the treatment group as a whole. The latter is based on average weekly attendance for the group of nine as a whole.

9. Comparing Pre-Treatment Attendance With Attendance During Treatment

The social worker then compares the pre-treatment findings with those attained during treatment. This is done for each youngster and for the group as a whole. Seven out of nine of the youngsters show improved attendance rates. Four out of the seven show statistically significant improvement. The group taken as a whole, however, does not.

10. Collecting Supportive Data

In a final session with the youngsters, the social worker has them talk about their feelings about school and makes note of those youngsters who appear to be expressing less fearful and more positive attitudes. Interviews are also conducted with parents to corroborate these impressions. In addition, these interviews are designed to determine whether the youngsters, or the parents are currently receiving any treatment elsewhere. Finally, information is gathered about the family's circumstances within the preceding couple of months.

The social worker discovers that the parents of three out of four of the youngsters who have made statistically significant improvements in attendance are also in therapy. All the parents, however, indicate that their children seem to have more positive attitudes toward school.

11. Taking Post-Treatment Measures

After treatment has terminated, the social worker keeps track of the individual and group weekly attendance scores for the following two months.

12. Comparing Attendance Scores During and After Treatment

A visual and statistical comparison of the individual and group attendance scores during and after treatment reveals that those children whose parents are in treatment continue to improve, whereas, there has been a slight decline for those children whose parents were not. This decline, however is not statistically significant. The post-treatment scores for the group as a whole appear to be stabilized and are not significantly different from the "baseline" derived during treatment.

13. Comparing Attendance Records for Each Clinical Phase

On the basis of comparisons made for each clinical phase, for each child, and for the treatment group as a whole, the social worker determines that the group technique is an effective one, but it is most effective in conjunction with parental receipt of treatment. As a result, s/he decides to try another similar group but to simultaneously refer the parents of the children in the new group to a cooperating family service agency in the community for casework help.

EXERCISE

Specify one treatment objective for an individual or group that can be evaluated by an interrupted time-series design. Describe how you would implement such a design and the comparisons you would make to determine how effective treatment has been.

SELECTED BIBLIOGRAPHY

Campbell, Donald T. and Julian C. Stanley, *Exp Quasi-Experimental Designs for Research* (Chicago: Ra 1966), pp. 5–6, and 37–42.

Caporaso, James A. and Leslie L. Roos, Jr., eds., *Qu tal Approaches* (Evanston, Ill.: Northwestern Univ 1973), pp. 9–35.

Carter, Robert, "Internal Validity in Intensive Expe 11 pp., and "Designs and Data Patterns in Inte mentation (Part 1)," 12 pp, Course Monographs, R terpersonal Influence, University of Michigan, Sch Work, Ann Arbor, 1972.

Epstein, Irwin and Tony Tripodi, *Research Technique Planning, Monitoring, and Evaluation* (New York: Co versity Press, 1977), pp. 117–30.

Gottman, John M. and Sandra R. Leiblum, *How T therapy and How To Evaluate It* (New York: Holt, F Winston, 1974), pp. 138–51 and 158–73.

Hersen, Michel and David H. Barlow, *Single Case Designs* (New York: Pergamon, 1976), pp. 70–91 an

Jayaratne, Srinika and Rona L. Levy, *Empirical Cli* (New York: Columbia University Press, 1979), pp.

Thomas, Edwin J., "Uses of Research Methods in I Practice", in Norman A. Polansky, ed., *Social Work* ed.; Chicago: University of Chicago Press, 1975), pp

other variations on the interrupted time-series design can be found in Hersen and Barlow (1976), Thomas (1975), and in Jayaratne and Levy (1979).

Since the evaluative approaches mentioned above are all based on the interrupted time-series format, they are subject to the requirements and limitations of the basic design. Thus, effective implementation depends on the extent to which valid and reliable data are employed in the measurement process, and particularly on the demonstration of high test/retest reliability. In addition, the use of more complex design variations such as graduated designs, withdrawal designs and multiple baseline designs involves additional effort in order to produce knowledge which more closely approximates cause-effect knowledge. This extra effort may take more time or may make other demands which are not readily achievable in many clinical settings (Thomas 1978). However, these more rigorous designs need not be routinely implemented. Rather, they may be used judiciously, when there is a desire for greater certainty about the effectiveness of clinical interventions and when setting conditions permit. Moreover, knowledge of these design variations, and the principles which are implied within them can contribute to systematic thinking about clinical social work practice whether or not the research designs themselves are ever actually implemented.

RESEARCH DESIGN VARIATIONS AND CLINICAL DECISION-MAKING

As we indicated earlier, the design variations to be discussed here are refinements of the interrupted time-series design. When using this basic evaluative design, a statistically significant improvement from baseline through the treatment implementation phase with no significant deterioration in the follow-up evaluation would suggest a positive association between treatment and effectiveness. With interrupted time-series designs, most internal validity factors can be controlled (with the exception of contemporary history and maturation). The additional controls that are discussed strengthen the causal inferences that can be made.

Three refinements of the interrupted time-series design make it possible to control for contemporary history, maturation and the effects of multiple interventions. These are the graduated design, the withdrawal design, and the multiple baseline design. These variations are as much related to clinical decisions as they are to research considerations. So, for example, after an initial period of treatment, a clinical social worker may be faced with the option of continuing treatment in its present form; increasing the frequency or intensity of the treatment; adding a new intervention; or withdrawing treatment. In making these decisions, the clinician could certainly benefit from systematic information about the effects of the orginal intervention, the effects of increasing intervention, and/or the effects of decreasing intervention. In addition, the clinician would be interested in whether the gains that a client has made are generalizing to other areas of the client's life. Finally, one would want to know whether other comparable clients would make similar gains if they received the same interventions.

To assess the effectiveness of a continuous form of treatment, the interrupted time-series design would suffice. However, to systematically assess variations in treatment and to answer questions about the extent to which treatment gains can be generalized, one must turn to variations on and replications of interrupted time-series designs. Some of these design refinements, their uses and their limitations are discussed below.

GRADUATED DESIGNS

The *graduated design* is logically similar to the interrupted time-series design, but is geared to assessing the impact of increased or decreased intervention. In implementing this design, client stability or change is monitored during a baseline phase, during the initial treatment phase, and during the graduated treatment phase. Figure 12.1 represents an ideal data pattern for this design, with statistically significant decreases in the expression of client problems

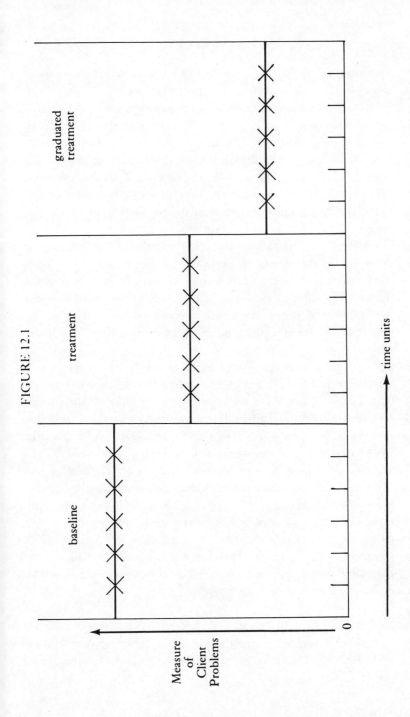

FIGURE 12.1

from baseline to the first treatment phase and from the first treatment phase to the graduated treatment phase.

Since the graduated design involves the assessment of two successive treatment phases, it is less likely that extrinsic changes in the client's life (contemporary history) or client maturation could account for the statistically significant shifts noted in figure 12.1 (Carter 1972). Hence the graduated design which produces an ideal data pattern provides greater certainty of a causal connection between treatment and outcome than would interrupted time-series design.

The graduated design is particularly useful when the clinician is interested in the effects of increasing treatment intensity. Treatment intensity can be operationalized in terms of variations in the duration of treatment sessions, the frequency of treatment sessions, the addition of a new treatment intervention, the degree of involvement of the clinician, and the degree of participation of the client.

The graduated design is least useful when the ideal data pattern referred to in figure 12.1 does not emerge. Under these conditions (for example, when there are no statistically significant differences between the first and second treatment phases), the knowledge produced by a graduated design offers no greater certainty than would an interrupted time-series design. Finally, graduated designs are difficult to implement simultaneously with more than one client. Ideally, simultaneous implementation would make possible aggregation of client data and generalizations about treatment effectiveness. In clinical situations, however, client treatment goals and treatment itself, are rarely the same from client to client and from therapist to therapist. In those unusual instances in which comparability does exist, however, graduated designs can be used to evaluate whole treatment programs.

WITHDRAWAL DESIGNS

Another device for testing the causal connection between clinical intervention and outcome is the *withdrawal design*. This variation on the interrupted time-series design involves the withdrawal of treatment after a statistically significant improvement has occurred. The client's moods, attitudes, and/or behaviors are then monitored to determine whether there has been a statistically significant regression to the baseline level during the period in which treatment is withdrawn. If this regression does occur, treatment is reintroduced. If a statistically significant improvement takes place, one can assert that cause-effect knowledge has been achieved and that positive client outcomes are clearly related to treatment.

Figure 12.2 shows the ideal data pattern in a withdrawal design. Here again the likelihood is greater than in the interrupted time-series design that client outcomes are the consequence of clinical intervention rather than of contemporary history or maturation (Carter 1972).

The chief limitation of the withdrawal design is that it depends on an ideal data pattern. It cannot be employed unless there has been a statistically significant regression to the baseline level after treatment has been withdrawn. Moreover, it cannot be employed if agency conditions or other factors make it impossible to reinstitute treatment. Finally, the design requires extensive monitoring of the client's progress during the various phases of treatment and nontreatment. Such long-term monitoring is often difficult to achieve. For selected clients (particularly those with recurring problems and long-term relationships with the agency), a withdrawal design may be feasible. For purposes of program evaluation, however, the withdrawal design is impractical.

MULTIPLE BASELINE DESIGNS

Multiple baseline designs are research devices to determine whether the beneficial effects of treatment with a client are generalizable to other areas of the client's life or to other clients receiving similar treatment. For example, a client may be receiving treatment primarily focussed on improving his/her relationships with co-workers. A baseline is constructed to monitor improvement in his/her relationships on the job. In addition, however, a baseline is

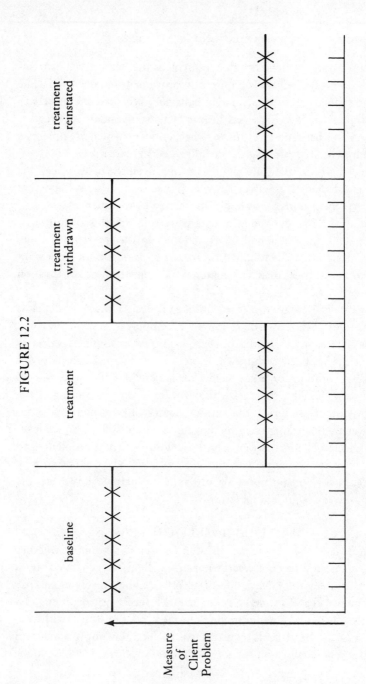

FIGURE 12.2

baseline   treatment   treatment
                         withdrawn

treatment
reinstated

Measure
of
Client
Problem

→ time units

constructed to assess changes in the client's relationship with his/her spouse. If there are statistically significant improvements in relationships at work and at home then the assumption is made that the beneficial effects of treatment have generalized beyond the work site.

The ideal data pattern for a multiple baseline design of two situations with a single client is illustrated in figure 12.3. To properly employ this design variation, one must first demonstrate that the two baselines are independent of each other. In other words, one would have to show that there was not a strong correlation between the clients behaviors, attitudes or moods in the different situations prior to intervention. Second, one must show that focussing on treatment in one situation does not alter the behavior in another. For example, while treatment is focussed on situation A in figure 12.3, it is not directed to situation B which shows no changes. Third, treatment is focused on situation B and desirable changes are observed. Finally, after treatment, both situations should have maintained their desirable changes at follow-up. These requirements make this design impractical in many treatment contexts in which client problems are likely to be highly interrelated.

The time lagged control feature of the multiple baseline design can be employed sequentially with more than one client. It requires: (1) at least two clients with similar treatment objectives, (2) at least two clients who are to receive similar treatment interventions, and (3) at least one of the clients on a waiting list. In this design, treatment takes place sequentially, with treatment beginning with the second client only after a statistically significant improvement has been demonstrated with the first client. The ideal data pattern for this design is demonstrated in figure 12.4.

Time-lagged control group designs are most practical in short-term intervention situations with highly specific treatment goals. Thus, they lend themselves to educational settings most readily. They are also employed in program evaluations in agencies in which there are large numbers of similar clients and insufficient resources to serve them all at once (Epstein and Tripodi 1977: ch. 13).

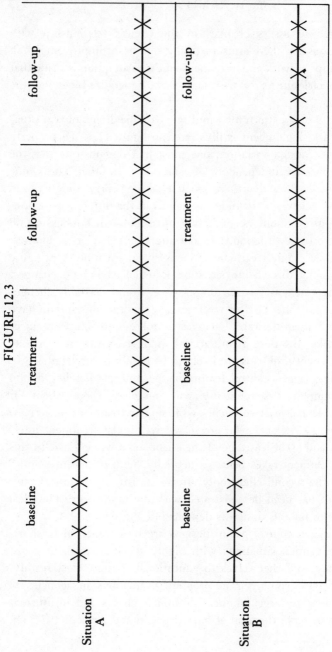

FIGURE 12.3

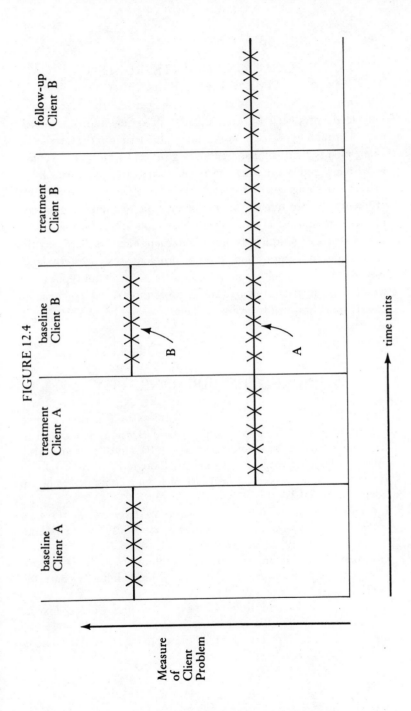

FIGURE 12.4

REPLICATIONS OF INTERRUPTED
TIME-SERIES DESIGNS

Perhaps the simplest strategy for increasing the certainty of knowledge produced by interrupted time-series studies is *replication*. Through repeatedly doing interrupted time-series studies of single clients, with similar treatment goals and similar intervention approaches and comparing the results, one can accumulate information regarding whether interventions are effective with a variety of clients. Before moving to this broad type of inquiry, however, Hersen and Barlow (1976) suggest that replications be made with clients that are as similar as possible to each other on characteristics such as family composition, type of problem, sex, age, ethnicity, and the like. As a rule of thumb, 3 out of 4 successful replications would indicate that the treatment procedures used are generalizeable to a comparable group of clients.

SELECTED BIBLIOGRAPHY

Carter, Robert, "Designs and Data Patterns in Intensive Experimentation (Part II Reversal Designs)," and "Designs and Data Patterns in Intensive Experimentation (Part III Graduated and Multiple Baseline Designs)," Course Monographs, Research in Interpersonal Influence, Social Work 683, University of Michigan, School of Social Work, 1972.

Epstein, Irwin and Tony Tripodi, *Research Techniques for Program Planning, Monitoring, and Evaluation* (New York: Columbia University Press, 1977), pp. 162–73.

Gottman, John M. and Sandra R. Leiblum, *How To Do Psychotherapy and How To Evaluate It* (New York: Holt, Rinehart and Winston, 1974), pp. 139–51.

Jayaratne, Srinika and Rona L. Levy, *Empirical Clinical Practice* (New York: Columbia University Press, 1979), pp. 137–312.

Hersen, Michel and David H. Barlow, *Single Case Experimental*

Designs (New York: Pergamon Press, 1976), pp. 225–64 and 317–56.

Kazdin, Alan E., "Methodological and Interpretive Problems of Single-Case Experimental Designs, *Journal of Consulting and Clinical Psychology* (August 1978), 46(4):629–42.

Mahoney, Michael J., "Experimental Methods and Outcome Evaluation," *Journal of Consulting and Clinical Psychology* (August 1978), 46(4):660–72.

Thomas, Edwin J., "Uses of Research Methods in Interpersonal Practice," in Norman A. Polansky, ed., *Social Work Research* (rev. ed.; Chicago: University of Chicago Press, 1975), pp. 254–83.

—— "Research and Service in Single-Case Experimentation: Conflicts and Choices," *Social Work Research and Abstracts* (Winter 1978), 14(4):20–31.

POSTSCRIPT

We have attempted to show how research concepts, techniques, and knowledge can be applied to clinical social work practice. More specifically, we have tried to show that research procedures can be employed as practice tools, particularly for obtaining information relevant to diagnostic assessment, treatment implementation, and evaluation. Although we divided treatment heuristically into the foregoing three phases, we recognize that they are interrelated in practice. Moreover, the research techniques introduced in the context of any one of these phases might just as easily have been applied to one of the others. So, for example, rating scales can be used in diagnostic assessment, treatment monitoring, and in evaluation of treatment effectiveness. Consequently, a complete understanding of the book requires flexible application of the research concepts and techniques discussed to different areas of clinical decision-making.

SOME REMINDERS

This book is geared to social work students and to practitioners who do not have a high level of research sophistication. Accordingly, we have presented relatively simple research concepts and techniques that can easily be mastered. In trying to present this material in understandable and approachable form (no simple task given the negative attitudes that so many social workers have toward research), it is inevitable that we will be accused of oversimplifying research by some of our researcher colleagues. Clinicians also may accuse us of oversimplifying clinical issues.

Our intent has not been to oversimplify. Rather, it has been to link some very basic research concepts with the fundamentals of clinical practice. Similarly, the bibliographies at the end of each chapter are selective. They provide the reader with some basic sources. Rather than being exhaustive and redundant, they are representative. Finally, they were selected with a mind to what consumers without extensive research training could read and understand. Thus far, feedback from students and practitioners who have been exposed to the contents of this book in manuscript form has been encouraging.

Perhaps the most difficult idea that we have tried to get across is that one can apply the logic of research to clinical practice. In other words, one can use research thinking for purposes other than research. In this vein, we hope our book has made a contribution to bringing research and clinical social work practice closer together.

INDEX